CW01020031

Trinity Mirror Media

Compiled by: Alan Jewell
Design & Production: Zoe Bevan, Colin Harrison
Cover Design: Rick Cooke

Pictures copyright: Mirrorpix, Liverpool Daily Post & Echo,
National Museums Liverpool, National Maritime Museum,
Ifremer, Press Association, Cunard

Liverpool Daily Post & Echo Image Archive:
Brian Johnston

Every effort has been made to acknowledge
copyright of imagery.

Special thanks to National Museums Liverpool

Executive Editor: Ken Rogers
Senior Editor: Steve Hanrahan
Editor: Paul Dove
Senior Art Editor: Rick Cooke
Trinity Mirror Media Marketing Executive: Claire Brown
Sales and Marketing Manager: Elizabeth Morgan
Sales and Marketing Assistant: Karen Cadman

Printed by William Gibbons

CONTENTS

WHEN THE UNTHINKABLE HAPPENED TO THE UNSINKABLE

THE DISASTER THAT BEFELL TITANIC WAS ONE OF THE MOST SHOCKING EVENTS OF THE 20TH CENTURY. THE TRIUMPH OF ITS CONSTRUCTION WAS FOLLOWED BY THE TRAGEDY OF ITS SINKING, AS OVER 1,500 PEOPLE DIED IN HIGHLY CONTROVERSIAL CIRCUMSTANCES

A CENTURY after she met her doom, Titanic is still the greatest legend in maritime history.

No ship has ever planted herself so firmly within the national consciousness. She remains a source of wonder and mystery, a liner of unprecedented scale and luxury. Nobody had ever travelled in such style and comfort – at least until that fateful encounter with the iceberg.

Facts and myths are difficult to distinguish about what occurred when she went down. The story goes that Titanic's band played 'Nearer, My God, To Thee' as the ship disappeared below the waves, but is it true? Given the conflicting accounts and the time lapse since the incident, we will surely never know.

Left: Captain Smith with Lord Pirrie, the chairman of Harland and Wolff

Below: The terrible news reaches Britain

Above: An unused first-class ticket

Standing tall, in all her glory, but disaster lay ahead

Titanic is always with us. The story is referenced so often in modern life, it's hard to believe that people cannot be aware of what happened, at least on a basic level. It has been dramatised many times, and another big-budget production is due to be shown on ITV over the upcoming anniversary.

James Cameron's 1997 film was the most expensive movie ever made. The investment paid off as it became the highest grossing in history, at least until 2010, making $1.8million at the box office.

Cameron articulated its appeal thus: "The story could not have been written better. The juxtaposition of rich and poor, the gender roles played out unto death (women first), the stoicism and nobility of a bygone age, the magnificence of the great ship matched in scale only by the folly of the men who drove her hell-bent through the darkness. And above all the lissom: that life is uncertain, the future unknowable…the unthinkable possible."

Commissioned by the White Star Line, she was built at the Harland and Wolff shipyard in Belfast, a vast project that required the labour of 3,000 men over a two-year period between 1909 and 1911.

The success of her construction confirmed the coming of a new era of confidence and prosperity in Britain. A floating palace, she possessed three huge decks, a grand staircase, swimming pool, Turkish bath, smoking room, dining saloon, gymnasium, cafe, writing room and lounge. She was seen as indestructible, "practically unsinkable" as was claimed at the time.

White Star's preparations for the maiden voyage were directed from their Liverpool headquarters by Captain Charles Bartlett, their marine superintendent in the port, supported by colleagues there and in Southampton. These arrangements began well before the ship left Belfast with the selection of key officers and crew, involving many transfers of personnel from other White Star vessels, and the provision of a wide range of supplies and equipment. Their policy for the maiden voyage of big ships was to have their most experienced crew members operating them, which is why Captain Edward Smith was selected to take charge.

He was the foremost naval captain of the age, but, sadly, he would go down with his ship.

Titanic set sail from Southampton on April 10 1912 with 922 passengers on board. Bound for New York, she made stops at Cherbourg, France, and Queenstown (now renamed Cobh) in Ireland and the figure increased to 1,316. With the addition of the crew, she carried 2,208 in all.

It had been a pleasant, uneventful journey until late on April 14 when she reached icy waters off the coast of Newfoundland. Despite warnings through the day from other ships in the area about the presence of 'bergs, Titanic ploughed on and was actually travelling faster than at any stage since leaving Southampton.

An iceberg right in the path of the ship was spotted by one of the lookouts at 11.40pm on the 14th. Despite immediate warnings and an attempt at evasive action, a collision could not be avoided.

Although many on board were not aware anything had happened, there was a scraping sound on the starboard side and a 250-foot gash made in the hull. Water rushed into the forward compartments at a volume that meant Titanic could not survive.

It took a while before passengers became aware of the severity of the situation and many were reluctant, or even refused, to get into the lifeboats. To compound the situation, the execution of the evacuation was flawed, with many boats leaving Titanic with spaces still available. As the lifeboat capacity (1,178) was nowhere near enough to cover all those on board, these factors combined meant the number of deaths (1,503) was grotesquely high.

It took just over two-and-a-half-hours from the initial impact until Titanic eventually sank. A total of 705 people managed to survive, the majority of them women and children who had been given priority in the evacuation process. They were rescued in the early hours of the 15th by the Cunard liner Carpathia, which rushed to the scene when it picked up a distress message.

Carpathia's Captain, Arthur Henry Rostron, who showed great skill and courage in moving so quickly through vast ice-fields to rescue survivors, was later rewarded with a knighthood and the US Congressional Gold Medal. His fellow officers and crew members were also decorated with awards.

The late Ernest St Clair, from Liverpool, was a steward on Carpathia. In an interview in 1982, he recalled: "Our wireless operator, by a mere freak of fate, had put on his headphones for a moment before going off duty and heard the dreaded call from the Titanic on her maiden and last voyage.

"Our ship was diverted from her course and every available bit of steam was used to go at full speed. There was a scramble to volunteer in the rescue and we worked like demons in the biting wind, getting up blankets and swinging out the lifeboats.

"Then in the greying dawn we saw the light of a flare and we soon saw the pitiably few survivors aboard, guided by the rockets we had sent up."

Apart from the insufficient lifeboats, there was plenty of controversy in the aftermath, particularly surrounding the SS Californian, a Leyland Line steamship. It was claimed that lights seen from Titanic as it listed on the waves came from the Californian, but its Captain, Stanley Lord, maintained his ship was too far away to get to the stricken ship in time. Whatever the reality, Lord's reputation took a battering as he was criticised in the official US and British inquiries.

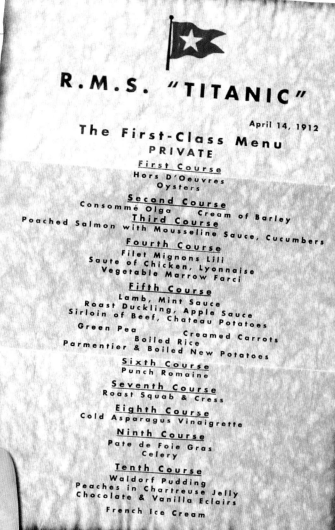

R.M.S. "TITANIC"

The First-Class Menu
April 14, 1912

PRIVATE

First Course
Hors D'Oeuvres
Oysters

Second Course
Consommé Olga   Cream of Barley

Third Course
Poached Salmon with Mousseline Sauce, Cucumbers

Fourth Course
Filet Mignons Lili
Saute of Chicken, Lyonnaise
Vegetable Marrow Farci

Fifth Course
Lamb, Mint Sauce
Roast Duckling, Apple Sauce
Sirloin of Beef, Chateau Potatoes
Green Pea   Creamed Carrots
Boiled Rice
Parmentier & Boiled New Potatoes

Sixth Course
Punch Romaine

Seventh Course
Roast Squab & Cress

Eighth Course
Cold Asparagus Vinaigrette

Ninth Course
Pate de Foie Gras
Celery

Tenth Course
Waldorf Pudding
Peaches in Chartreuse Jelly
Chocolate & Vanilla Eclairs
French Ice Cream

Above and left: The first and third-class menus for April 14, the day that Titanic struck the iceberg

WHITE STAR LINE.

R.M.S. "TITANIC."   APRIL 14, 1912.

THIRD CLASS.

BREAKFAST.
Oatmeal Porridge & Milk
Smoked Herrings, Jacket Potatoes
Ham & Eggs
Fresh Bread & Butter
Marmalade   Swedish Bread
Tea   Coffee

DINNER.
Rice Soup
Fresh Bread   Cabin Biscuits
Roast Beef, Brown Gravy
Sweet Corn   Boiled Potatoes
Plum Pudding, Sweet Sauce
Fruit

TEA.
Cold Meat
Cheese   Pickles
Fresh Bread & Butter
Stewed Figs & Rice
Tea

SUPPER.
Gruel   Cabin Biscuits   Cheese
Any complaint respecting the Food supplied, want of attention or incivility, should be at once reported to the Purser or Chief Steward. For purposes of identification, each Steward wears a numbered badge on the arm.

Others who came in for criticism included Bruce Ismay, the chairman of the White Star Line, who was accused of behaving selfishly by boarding the penultimate lifeboat, while women and children remained on the ship.

Titanic was one of three sister ships built on a grand scale. Olympic had a long career, operating the Southampton to New York route between 1911 and 1935 and acting as a troopship during the First World War. She earned the nickname 'Old Reliable' before being broken up in 1937. Britannic wasn't so lucky – she sank after hitting a German mine during the war in 1916.

Until late on Thursday April 18, when Carpathia arrived in New York, many of the news reports circulating on both sides of the Atlantic about Titanic's fate were unclear and contradictory.

When news first came through of the catastrophe that had befallen Titanic, worried crowds besieged White Star's offices in Southampton, London and Liverpool, anxiously waiting for news of those who had lived and died.

Facts were scarce because wireless could only flash short messages across short distances and those searching for survivors were too busy to send detailed reports. Officials in Liverpool were said to have shouted what little news they had from a first floor window to the crowds below.

The scenes were particularly desperate in Southampton, from where the majority of the crew hailed. It was said that there was not a family in the city or surrounding area who did not lose a relative in friend.

In many cases the only breadwinner was lost, while in some streets every house was represented on board, particularly in poorer areas where firemen and seafarers lived in large numbers.

Below: A stroll along the second-class promenade deck, while, above, extreme comfort in a first-class bedroom

The builder's model of Titanic, which is displayed in the Merseyside Maritime Museum

Launch

OF

White Star Royal Mail Triple-Screw Steamer

"TITANIC"

At BELFAST,

Wednesday, 31st May, 1911, at 12·15 p.m.

Admit Bearer.

Left: A ticket for the launch of Titanic

Liverpool was also hit hard. Available evidence suggests that the total number of crew and associated staff who sailed on Titanic's maiden voyage was 892. Of these, at least 114 were people with Liverpool backgrounds or strong associations with the city and vicinity. Most of the crew from the area died, including chief engineer Joseph Bell and several others from the engine room and stokeholds, who died trying to keep the ship afloat and illuminated as long as possible.

Memorial services were held across the country in the weeks afterwards as the dead were mourned, most notably at St Paul's Cathedral. Relief funds were set up to help bereaved families. Above all, it was a human tragedy.

APRIL 17, 1912

Below: Reginald Lee, a
lookout on Titanic, leaves
the Celtic at Liverpool on
May 6, 1912

Above: Mail is delivered to
the crew and passengers

WHITE STAR – AN ICON OF THE SEAS

THE COMPANY THAT CREATED TITANIC BUILT A SHIPPING EMPIRE THROUGH THE NORTH ATLANTIC ROUTES IN THE LATE 19TH CENTURY. WHITE STAR'S AMBITION KNEW NO BOUNDS

ONE of the most famous maritime companies made their name as the age of mass sea travel was dawning but the shadow of the Titanic will always loom over the White Star Line.

The organisation in its most famous form came into being in 1868 over a game of billiards.

Thomas Henry Ismay was a director of the National Line, based in Water Street, in Liverpool.

He was invited to Broughton Hall, a Gothic house built by Gustav Christian Schwabe in 1860. Schwabe, originally from Hamburg, had become a prominent Liverpool merchant. Schwabe had also invited his nephew, Gustav Wolff, to join them for a convivial dinner.

After the meal, a deal was struck. Ismay agreed to have ships built at Harland and Wolff in Belfast and in return Schwabe pledged to finance a company called the Oceanic Steam Navigation Company. This later became the White Star Line.

It was agreed that Harland and Wolff would not build any vessels for any of Ismay's rivals. The first orders were made in 1869.

Thomas Ismay, whose father, Joseph, was a small-time boat-builder in Maryport, Cumberland, was an ambitious man who settled in Liverpool and built up his shipping empire. By the early 1870s, his White Star line was challenging Cunard on the Atlantic routes after setting up a New York-Liverpool service (with a stop at Queenstown) in 1871

The company began with six ships, Oceanic, Atlantic, Baltic, Republic, Celtic and Adriatic. As can be seen from the list, White Star's theme was to give its ships names ended in 'ic'.

The line also adopted a buff funnel with a black top as a distinguishing feature of its ships, as well as the iconic flag – a white star on a red background.

There was an early disaster when Atlantic sank off the coast of Nova Scotia, resulting in the loss of 535 lives, but the company went from strength to strength.

During the late 19th century, White Star operated many of the most famous ships of the time, including Britannic, Germanic, Teutonic and Majestic. Initially their vessels were built with speed in mind but as the 20th century dawned the focus turned to scale and luxury.

Ismay died a wealthy many in 1899 after a comfortable existence in Thurstaston, Wirral. His son, J. Bruce Ismay, succeeded him as chairman and went on to become a notorious figure in the Titanic tragedy.

Bruce Ismay, the chairman of White Star, whose reputation was scarred forever after he survived the disaster by climbing aboard the penultimate lifeboat

Bruce was born in 1862. The J stood for Joseph after his grandfather. While Thomas Ismay started work at 16 in the shipyards, Bruce had a much more privileged upbringing. Educated at Harrow, he excelled at sport. He returned to Liverpool to learn the business in his father's shipping office. After a brief apprenticeship, he was appointed the company's representative in New York. In 1888 he married an American heiress before returning to England as a White Star director four years later.

One of Bruce's first major acts was to build four ocean liners to surpass the Oceanic, which was commissioned by his father just before his death and was, at the time, the largest ship in the world. The 'Big Four' were RMS Celtic, RMS Cedric, RMS Baltic and RMS Adriatic.

In 1902 American financier JP Morgan created the International Mercantile Marine Company (IMMC) by purchasing a number of major US and British shipping lines. Ismay agreed to sell White Star to Morgan. In return, Ismay was

A modern view of Albion House,
known as the White Star
building, in Liverpool city centre

A promotional calendar advertising White Star Line services

appointed chairman and managing director of the new organisation, of which White Star was now a subsidiary.

The British government was shaken by White Star falling into American hands and blocked the sale of Cunard to Morgan. Loans were provided to Cunard, which enabled them to build two large and fast ships – Lusitania and Mauritania.

White Star knew they couldn't compete speed-wise and hit on a plan to build three liners of unparalleled luxury. In 1907 Ismay met Lord Pirrie of Harland and Wolff to discuss their response and the result of their talks was three floating palaces – sister ships Olympic, Britannic and Titanic.

In the same year White Star transferred its main New York service from Liverpool to Southampton. This was at least partly due to competition from Cunard liners Lusitania and Mauritania, both of which sailed from Liverpool from that year. However, White Star's headquarters remained in Liverpool and major decisions continued to be made from the city's office.

Ismay would sometimes accompany his ships on their maiden voyage, and did so when Titanic took to the seas. He was heavily criticised in the American and British press for escaping the doomed liner in collapsible boat 'C' (the penultimate lifeboat to be launched) while women and children were still on board.

It is said that after she struck the iceberg, he spent 90 minutes urging, "Women and children first," but the stigma of the disaster blighted his life subsequently and he was dubbed J 'Brute' Ismay.

Ismay shunned public life from this point and felt uncomfortable whenver he travelled up to Liverpool from London, reserving a whole compartment for himself when he took the train to avoid public abuse.

As for White Star, it was sold by IMMC to the Royal Mail Steam Packet Company (RMSPC) in 1927 but five years later RMSPC was liquidated after running into financial trouble. A new company, Royal Mail Lines Limited, took over the lines, including White Star.

In 1933, in the depths of the Great Depression, White Star and Cunard were in financial strife. The British government provided financial assistance on the condition that they merged their North Atlantic operations. Cunard White Star Limited officially came into existence in May 1934. Cunard was the dominant partner and the name reverted to 'Cunard' in 1949.

The White Star Line's London, Liverpool and Southampton offices, named Oceanic House, Albion House and Canute Chambers respectively, still exist today. Oceanic House is home to a restaurant and commercial offices, while Albion House was, in January 2012, available for let. Canute Chambers is also an office building.

Titanic's sister ship, the Olympic,
arriving in Southampton

The cabinet shop at Harland and Wolff in 1899. Skilled craftsmen were required to make the huge quantities of wooden furnishings and fittings in the cabins and public rooms of large liners. The bowler-hatted man in the foreground is probably the shop foreman

BUILDING A LEGEND

IT TOOK JUST OVER TWO YEARS TO BUILD TITANIC AT THE HARLAND AND WOLFF SHIPYARD IN BELFAST, A TASK THAT REQUIRED THE LABOUR OF 3,000 MEN AND THREE MILLION RIVETS

CONSTRUCTING the Titanic was an epic project requiring enormous financial resources and man-power at the Belfast shipyards of Harland and Wolff.

As has already been documented, Titanic and her sister ships Olympic and Britannic were built by White Star Line as a response to Cunard's super-fast liners Lusitania and Mauritania.

There was no intention to compete with the speed of Cunard's ships, but Bruce Ismay, chairman of White Star, and Lord Pirrie, of Harland and Wolff, wanted to build new liners of unprecedented size and luxury, but of moderate speed.

Work began first on the Olympic, whose keel was laid on December 16 1908 at slip no. 2 at Queen's Island, Belfast She was launched 22 months later on October 20 1910.

Titanic's keel was laid on March 22 1909 at slip no. 3 at Queen's Island. She was launched 26 months later on May 31 1911.

The two enormous hulls were built side by side, in adjacent slipways. On completion, Titanic, with an overall length of 882 feet 9 inches, was three inches longer than the Olympic.

Titanic's gross tonnage was 46,328, she was 92 feet wide with eight decks rising to the height of an 11-storey building.

The gantry used in the construction was 220 feet high, the largest in the world at the time. Harland and Wolff employed 14,000 men and 3,000 of them laboured for two years to complete Titanic. Two workers lost their lives during this period, which was actually fewer than would be expected for a project of this scale.

There were three million rivets used and 15 horses were required to pull just one of Titanic's 15-ton anchors through Belfast to the shipyard.

The final cost was £1.5m, a vast sum 100 years ago., and she could reach a top speed of 23 knots.

Titanic Statistics:

PASSENGER capacity: 1,034 in first class,
520 in second and 1,022 in third
Crew: 900
Certified to carry: 3,547 passengers and crew
Lifeboat capacity: 1,178 people

10,000 lightbulbs
29 boilers
159 furnaces
8,000 tons of coal

20 lifeboats
3,560 lifejackets
48 ringbuoys

8,000 eiderdown quilts
15,000 single sheets
3,000 doubles and 7,500 blankets
44,000 towels

Stores included:
75,000lbs fresh meat
11,000lbs fish
25,000lbs of poultry and game
40 tons of potatoes
800 bundles of fresh asparagus
250 barrels of flour
35,000 fresh eggs
7,000 lettuces
3,500 onions

12,000 dinner plates
500 salad bowls
9,000 cups and saucers
2,400 tea and coffee pots
1,500 champagne glasses
8,000 cigars
6,000 tablecloths
8,000 sets of cutlery
45,000 table napkins

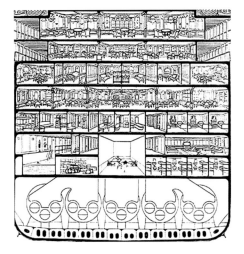

Designers deep in thought in the drawing office in 1912. The high ceiling and large number of windows allow for good use of natural light

Three loftsmen are chalking the lines of a ship on portable wooden flooring, full size for cross section and quarter scale for length, in order to determine the precise shapes needed for the steel frames, circa 1910

The great gantry used to construct Titanic. This image shows the enormous scale of the ship, which provides a contrast with the traditional wooden schooner in the foreground

Fitting the
tailshaft was
a precarious
operation

Incredibly, 15
horses were
required to pull
the anchors to
the shipyard

Titanic, shortly before its launch, attracting the attention of curious onlookers

An intimidating sight, ready to leave port

Titanic takes to the seas for trials before the maiden voyage

COUNTDOWN TO DISASTER

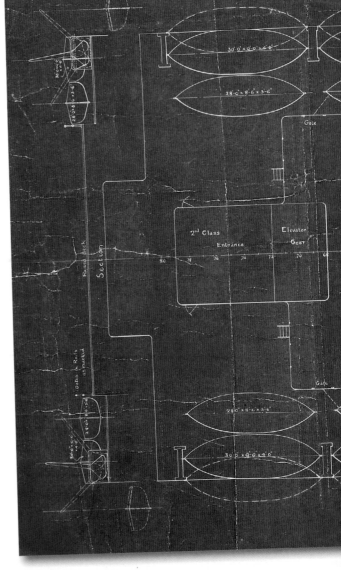

EVERTHING APPEARED TO BE GOING
SMOOTHLY ON THE MAIDEN VOYAGE, UNTIL
A BLACK MASS LOOMED INTO VIEW

IT was a cold but still day on April 14 1912. The Titanic was approaching 'The Corner', a great underwater plateau off the coast of Newfoundland.

Since setting sail on the 10th, the voyage had been favoured by calm seas and clear weather and proceeded in a largely uneventful manner.

However, in 1912 an unusually large amount of ice had drifted further south than usual. Icebergs had been reported coming towards the shipping lanes. For this reason, on the 14th Captain Smith altered course to travel 25 miles further south.

Ships in the area were radioing ice warnings to each other. As she steamed towards the location, the Titanic started to receive these warnings, too.

There was a message from White Star steamer Baltic at 1.42pm, which Captain Smith passed to White Star chairman Bruce Ismay without comment. Ismay put it in his pocket, where it stayed for five and a half hours until he belatedly posted it on the bridge.

The two lookouts in the crow's nest, Archie Jewell and George Symons, were following a special order to keep watch for ice. The night was clear, the surface calm and the sky was dotted with bright stars.

At 7.30pm there was an ice warning from Californian, reporting three large 'bergs about 19 miles north of Titanic's location.

Two hours later Captain Smith retired for the night, after checking with First Officer Charles Lightoller on conditions.

At 9.40pm the steamer Mesaba sent the sixth ice message of the day, warning of "much heavy pack ice and great number large icebergs". Busy with other transmissions, including private messages, the wireless operator failed to send the warning to the bridge. The Titanic continued at 22 1/2 knots, the fastest speed it had recorded, with officers reasoning that the clear night would allow plenty of time in which to sight ice.

At 11.40pm, lookout Fred Fleet spotted a black object about 500 yards ahead and immediately rang the warning bell three times, then telephoned Sixth Officer Moody on the bridge to confirm what he had seen and shouted: "Iceberg, right ahead".

Chief Officer William Murdoch ordered the ship "hard a-starboard". A collision seemed inevitable but at the last minute the ship's brow swung left and the iceberg passed along the right side of the ship.

The lookouts breathed a sigh of relief but an almost imperceptible grind and slight shudder, heard by some of the ship's sleepy passengers, hid a greater damage.

Below the waterline the 'berg had sheared a 250-foot gash in the hull, its pressure enough to open the inch-thick plates. The contact doomed the ship.

Captain Smith had felt the collision and had rushed down to the chart room to find out what had happened. The watertight doors had been closed as soon as a collision seemed imminent but the 'berg had badly damaged five out of six compartments. Water was rushing into the boiler rooms.

The engines were stopped and by 11.50 water was already 14 feet above the keel in the first five compartments. This ship's pumps could not cope with such a rate of inflow.

Captain Smith was informed by the ship's designer, Thomas Andrews, that Titanic had one and a half to two hours to live. At 12.05am he gave the order to prepare the lifeboats. Five minutes later he went back to the wireless room and told the operators to send a distress call.

Most people on board, whether crew or passengers, were asleep ▶

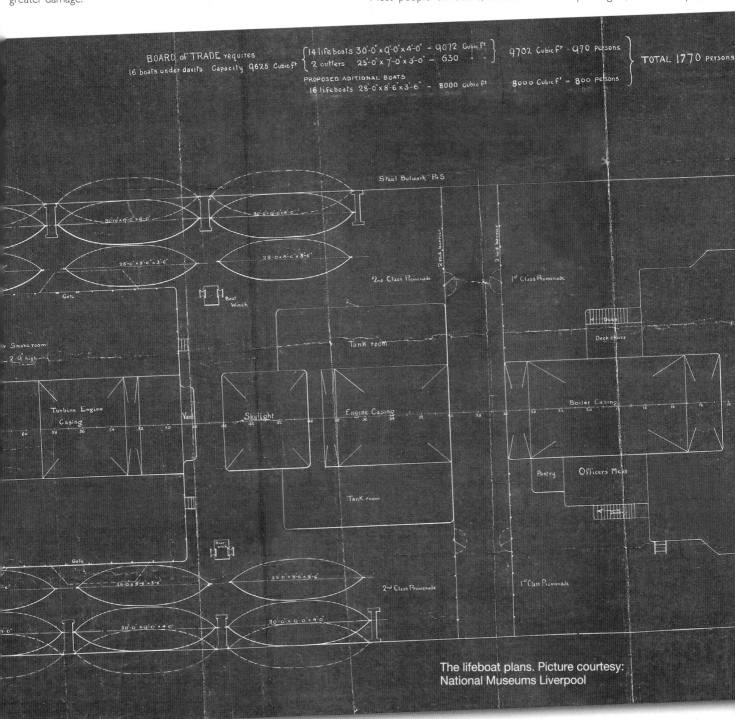

The lifeboat plans. Picture courtesy: National Museums Liverpool

Lord Pirrie, the chairman of Harland and Wolff, with Bruce Ismay, who held the same position with the White Star Line

or preparing for bed at the time of the collision. Even when they were ordered to wear lifejackets, plenty wondered what all the fuss was about and were reluctant to leave the warmth and comfort of the ship, believing it to be sturdier and safer than the lifeboats. The first rescue boat took only a few passengers.

It was only when emergency rockets were fired into the night air that some realised the Titanic was in trouble.

Several passengers and crew saw the lights of another ship, and thought it was within a few miles, but it never responded to wireless transmissions, rockets or a Morse lamp message. This would prove hugely controversial in the aftermath, as many believed it to be the Californian. It disappeared from view before Titanic sank and the mystery ship has never been properly accounted for.

At 12.25am Cunard's Carpathia received a distress signal shortly before its sole radio operator retired for the night. It was 58 miles south-east of Titanic and immediately headed for the stricken ship.

Within 10 minutes lifeboat no. 7 was lowered into the water. Despite a capacity of 65, only 28 were on board. Boat no. 1, with a capacity of 40, only had 12 aboard.

As the rockets soared into the sky, and Titanic became ever more unstable, the realisation gradually dawned among hitherto blase passengers that she was in serious trouble. After 1am Fifth Officer Harold Lowe was brandishing his gun to deter men from rushing boat no. 14, in defiance of the order "women and children first".

Bruce Ismay helped to fill the boats on starboard for over an hour, until, at about 1.40am, he was overseeing the final boat on that side. With no response to his calls for more women and children to fill available space, he climbed aboard as it was lowered, an action that led to wounding criticism, which haunted him for the rest of his life.

Collapsible boat D was the last rescue boat to be lowered around 2am. The people still on board tried to walk or crawl along the steeply sloping deck as the stern rose higher into the air. The noise was loud as boilers

Titanic and the steamer New York almost collided as the liner set off from Southampton. The turbulence from Titanic caused the smaller ship to break away from her moorings

came loose from their seatings, glass and china smashed, and coal, luggage and furniture all rolled forward. Those who remained on the ship lost their footing as the Titanic rose to an almost vertical position and waves crashed through the deck.

The lights flickered as the ship broke in two and slipped below the surface – the engineers who had been trying to keep the lights working to the last possible moment in the hope of rescue went down at their posts. The lights went out at 2.18am and two minutes later it was gone.

The ordeal wasn't over for hundreds of passengers who were struggling for breath in the icy waters until they knew the lifeboats wouldn't be coming back for them because of a fear of being swamped. Their cries for help gradually diminished while the survivors in the boats waited for help.

The Carpathia arrived just after 4am, two hours after the ship went down and just in time for those in the lifeboats as a wind had started to blow, creating waves that threatened to swamp them, while the effects of exposure were taking hold. Around 8.30am, after taking 705 survivors on board, she left the tragic site for New York.

The telegram sent by Bruce Ismay from on board the rescue ship Carpathia, confirming that Titanic had sunk, resulting in a significant loss of life. Picture courtesy: National Museums Liverpool

The Daily Mirror

THE MORNING JOURNAL WITH THE SECOND LARGEST NET SALE.

No. 2,645. Registered at the G.P.O. as a Newspaper. TUESDAY, APRIL 16, 1912 One Halfpenny.

DISASTER TO THE TITANIC: WORLD'S LARGEST SHIP COLLIDES WITH AN ICEBERG IN THE ATLANTIC DURING HER MAIDEN VOYAGE.

Disaster, it was reported yesterday, has overtaken the great steamer Titanic, the largest and most luxuriously appointed vessel afloat. The liner, which is the latest addition to the White Star fleet, left Southampton last Wednesday on her maiden voyage to New York, and was in the vicinity of the Newfoundland banks, to the south of Cape Race, when she struck an iceberg, an ever-present peril in those latitudes at this time of the year. "Wireless" has again demonstrated its immense value, assistance being summoned by this means. The photograph shows the mighty vessel leaving Southampton on Wednesday.—(Daily Mirror photograph.)

HOW THE STORY UNFOLDED

FROM THE FIRST REPORTS OF THE TITANIC'S SINKING, WHICH INCORRECTLY CLAIMED ALL
PASSENGERS WERE SAFE, THE DAILY MIRROR TOLD EVERY DETAIL OF THE TRAGIC TALE

APRIL 16, 1912:

THE White Star liner Titanic, the greatest ship the world has ever known, has met with disaster on her maiden voyage.

She left Southampton on Wednesday last and carried about 2,300 passengers and crew on board, with 3,4000 sacks of mail.

On Sunday she came into collision with an iceberg, and immediately flashed out wireless messages for help.

Many steamers rushed to her aid, but her fate and that of the thousands on board remained in doubt on both sides of the Atlantic for many hours.

It was at length known that every soul was safe and that the vessel itself was proceeding to Halifax (Nova Scotia), towed by the Allan liner Virginian.

All her passengers had by that time been taken aboard two of the liners that hurried to the scene in reply to the wireless message.

DRAMATIC TELEGRAMS OF DISASTER

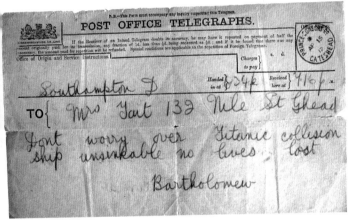

This reassuring telegram from a passenger proved premature

SO many and so conflicting were the reports that reached London yesterday concerning the fate of the Titanic that until detailed and definite tidings come to hand it is difficult to establish much more than the one all-important and outstanding fact that:

Every man, woman and child on the great liner is safe.

It would appear that once again the value to humanity of wireless telegraphy has been established, for at least five vessels are known to have hastened to the aid of the world's greatest ship when she flashed forth her appeal for help.

Thanks to the wonderful modern invention of wireless telegraphy, which ten years ago was unknown, the Titanic was able to flash messages over the ocean asking for aid.

The wireless signal for "assistance wanted" is now "SOS", the more familiar letters "CQD" having been abandoned because they led to confusion with other code signals.

As a result of these "SOS" messages, five ships went to the assistance of the Titanic – the Baltic and the Olympic, of the White Star Line; the Virginian and the Parisian, of the Allan Line, and the Cunarder Carpathia. The two last-named took off boat-loads of passengers.

Thus the passengers of the Titanic owe their safety to the invention of wireless, to the wondrous discovery of which it is due that every large liner is now in communication with any liner or battleship within hundreds of miles.

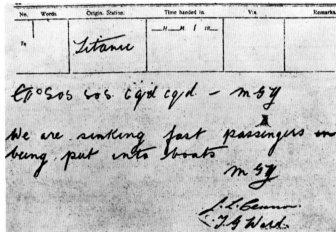

This was the last message received from Titanic as the desperate fate of the vessel became obvious to all on board

LINER THAT COST £1,500,000

TO be a passenger on the Titanic is to be resident in a luxurious town of over 3,000 inhabitants.

Life on board is life timed and arranged always with a view to comfort. Indeed, the passenger is almost safer when crossing the Atlantic than crossing a busy London thoroughfare.

Built by Messrs Harland and Wolff, the Titanic was launched in Belfast last year and cost £1,500,000.

The departure of the Titanic was perhaps somewhat ill-omened.

When leaving Southampton water, the suction from the big liner caused the hawsers holding the liner New York to the quayside to snap.

Immediately the stern of the New York began to drift towards the Titanic and a collision seemed inevitable.

The Titanic's engines were stopped and her three tugs cast off and went to the assistance of the New York.

Fortunately they were able to secure her to the quay again, but at one time only 15 feet separated the two vessels.

TWO MILE WALK ON BOARD

THERE are ten decks, and so complicated are the numerous passages, saloons and stairways that the passengers are provided with special guide maps in their staterooms to show them the way about.

One can go for a two-mile walk on the Titanic without going over the same point twice. Before sailing all the stewards of the liner had to be instructed in the geography of the giant ship, in order to learn the shortest route to various parts of the ship.

Like a smart seaside resort, the Titanic – infinitely more commodious than a hotel – provides every luxury a wealthy pleasure-loving public can wish.

A fully-equipped Turkish bath, squash court, swimming bath, gymnasium, ballroom and skating rink are some of these.

Glass enclosed 'sun parlours' are one of the most delightful innovations on the Titanic. Those who wish to take their meals on deck may visit the verandah cafe, made to represent those on the Riviera.

THE MAGNIFICENCE OF THE TITANIC: PORTRAITS OF

A photograph which gives an idea of the immense size of the Titanic. Her length over all is 882ft. 6in.—(Daily Mirror photograph.)

The cooling-room of the Turkish bath, one of the features of this sumptuous vessel. (Daily Mirror photograph.)

Colonel J. J. and Mrs. Astor.

Mr. Bruce Ismay.

Captain Smith, the com

Mr. Isidor Straus. Mrs. Cavendish. Mr. Clarence Moore. Major A. W. Butt. Mr. Charles M. Hays.

Photograph showing an iceberg as se

The passenger list of the Titanic includes the names of many well-known and distinguished people, portraits of a number of them appearing above. Mr. Bruce Ismay is chairman and managing director of the White Star Line and the eldest son of the founder of the concern. Captain Smith, in command of the Titanic, is one of the best-known ship

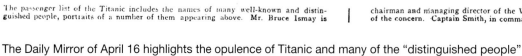

The Daily Mirror of April 16 highlights the opulence of Titanic and many of the "distinguished people" who were on board, at a stage when it was believed that all had survived

BLE PASSENGERS ON BOARD THE ILL-FATED VESSEL.

The Titanic and the New York within an ace of colliding with each other at Southampton on Wednesday. (*Daily Mirror* photograph.)

The Countess of Rothes.

Lord Ashburton.

Mirror photograph.)

A bed in one of the staterooms. The decorations are suggestive of some fine mansion. (*Daily Mirror* photograph.)

of a mail steamer in mid-ocean.

Mr. Benj. Guggenheim.

Miss Gladys Cherry.

Major A. Peuchen.

Miss Esther Bowen.

Mr. W. T. Stead.

rs on the North Atlantic. The Titanic, it will be remembered, narrowly escaped involved in a collision with the steamer New York at Southampton last W

day. The ropes holding the last-named vessel snapped, and she swung round, coming

The Daily Mirror

THE MORNING JOURNAL WITH THE SECOND LARGEST NET SALE.

No. 2,646. | Registered at the G.P.O. as a Newspaper. | April 17, 1912 | One Halfpenny.

PASSENGERS BOARDING THE TITANIC AT QUEENSTOWN AND SOME OF THE VICTIMS AND SURVIVORS OF HISTORY'S MOST TERRIBLE SHIPWRECK.

Chief Purser McElroy (clean-shaven) and Dr. W. F. N. O'Loughlin, the chief ship's surgeon. Both are missing. | Mr. K. H. Behr, the famous tennis player, saved. | Sir Cosmo Duff-Gordon, Bart., and his wife, who is better known as "Lucile." Both of them are reported saved.

Embarking on the Titanic at Queenstown last Thursday. This was the last port at which the ill-starred vessel called.

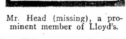

Mr. Daniel Marvin, reported missing, and his bride, who is saved. They were on a wedding trip. | Mr. Head (missing), a prominent member of Lloyd's. | Colonel J. J. and Mrs. Astor, returning from their honeymoon. She is saved, but his body has been picked up dead.

Queenstown was the last port at which the ill-fated Titanic called. She sailed on Thursday with the good wishes of everyone, only to founder less than a week afterwards. Two young brides, Mrs. J. J. Astor, the wife of the millionaire, and Mrs. Daniel Marvin, who had been spending their honeymoon in Europe, have been widowed by the disaster. Mr. Christopher Head was formerly Mayor of Chelsea. —(Daily Mirror, Dover-street Studios, and Russell.)

APRIL 17, 1912:

ONLY 868 ALIVE ON SUNKEN LINER

FURTHER news of the appalling disaster to the Titanic, the greatest ship that man has ever built, only adds fresh horrors.

It appears to be now established that 1,300 souls went to their deaths in the mid-Atlantic with the sinking of the liner.

The Cunard steamer Carpathia is steaming through fields of ice to New York, with 868 survivors on board – a tragic freight of widowed wives and fatherless children.

All hope is now abandoned that any other of the Titanic's 2,200 still lives. The Virginian and Parisian now report that they have picked up no one, and icy weather must have been fatal long since.

The mightiest of all craft that man, aided by all the resources of centuries of human knowledge, launched forth but a week on her maiden voyage now lies irrevocable, in two miles of all-devouring ocean, having met a mountain of ice in her passage from land to land.

Nothing now remains of that proud triumph of marine architecture, save masses of wreckage adrift among swirling ice floes.

It is good to know that the women and children were first to leave the doomed vessel. The best traditions of the sea were observed, as the Prime Minister feelingly told the House of Commons yesterday. The Carpathia is now making for New York with the 868 survivors, who alone call tell the tale of the midnight plunge into the angry whirlpool of ice, wreckage and drowning men with which the great ship went to her burial.

They alone can relate the bitter experiences of the wintry night spent in open boats on a lonely sea, of the waiting for morning and of the hope of rescue.

The wireless messages have told how in the darkness their crews had to guide the boats with the greatest caution to prevent their being jammed in the ice or overturned by the swirling foes, so that the heavily laden craft became widely separated from each other.

There followed hours of heart-breaking anguish before daylight came – and the Carpathia.

The Carpathia proceeded cautiously, sounding her fog-whistle almost continuously, until one after another she picked up the scattered lifeboats.

The White Star agents learned today from the Oceanic that all the Titanic's boats have been accounted for.

This, together with the abandonment of the long-cherished idea that the Virginian or Parisian might have picked up some additional survivors, has dispelled most of the hopes that the number of those saved may be increased beyond the pitiful 868.

The scene of the collision was in round figures 1,000 miles due east from New York and 600 miles south-east from Halifax (Nova Scotia).

Some of the survivors row towards Carpathia. On the opposite page, the Mirror front page from April 17 as the full scale of the disaster became clear. It accurately reported that JJ Astor, the richest passenger on board, had died

APRIL 18, 1912:

DEATH ROLL INCREASED BY 165: A WORLD WAITING

PATHETICALLY slowly, the Cunard liner Carpathia is nearing New York with her tragic load of widowed wives and orphaned children.

The eyes of the whole civilised world are following her as she ploughs through the ocean and icefields that fill the track.

For on board she carries all that are left of the 2,200 souls who set sail with such high hope last week for the maiden voyage of the Titanic, the greatest ship the world has ever known, man's supreme challenge to the powers of nature.

Now that ship has been shattered, and all that remains is sunk in 12,000ft of Atlantic Ocean. Of her human freight two in every three have perished; fathers, husbands, bread-winners.

And the world waits upon the Carpathia – waits to hear the appalling truth of that midnight crash when the 40,000-ton steamship met the mountain of ice.

Meanwhile, a funeral ship has left Halifax with a grim cargo of coffins, hoping to pick up the dead.

What is their number? No one yet knows for certain, but the most recent information seems to increase the death roll by over 160. Latest wireless reports speak of but 700 or 705 survivors on the Carpathia – formerly it was 868.

Estimates of the number of the dead must vary between 1,400 and 1,500, for not even the precise number of those on board when the Titanic sailed is yet definitely established.

Anxious crowds gather outside the White Star offices in Southampton. The newspaper poster seen in the centre of shot refers to the total solar eclipse of April 17

Night has fallen but the crowds remain in Southampton

TEAR-STAINED WOMEN WAIT FOR GOOD TIDINGS

HARROWING scenes at all the White Star Line offices. Anxiety, poignant and almost unrelieved, held two continents in grip all yesterday, waiting for tidings of the great ship which the sea had swallowed up.

At three great cities – London, New York and Paris – agonised relatives of those on board the Titanic thronged the offices of the White Star Company for news from those they feared lost.

Southampton, whence hail most of the 800 or 900 members of the crew, was a town of mourning and desolation, and in Liverpool and Belfast, too, keenest anxiety was felt on behalf of sons or husbands or fathers who went out on the great ship.

In London the saddest places of all were the offices of the White Star Line in Cockspur Street and Leadenhall Street.

Guarded by special constables, the offices were besieged all day by anxious relatives – sobbing women dressed in black seeking to learn the fate of their husbands, sons and loved ones.

It was a tragic scene, and as the heart-broken inquirers groped their way out of the doors, the golden spring sunshine which flooded Trafalgar Square only emphasised the contrast of life and death.

And it was the women who waited. For the only news of those saved was that stating that the majority are women and children. There was no news of the men – only silence.

All the shipping offices at Charing Cross and Cockspur Street had their flags flying at half mast.

From an early hour people began to arrive in taxicabs to seek the latest news.

Patiently the officials searched the lists again and again, but too often their reply was: "His name is not here."

One athletic girl in a Harris tweed costume was a pathetic figure. The news dashed her hopes, but she was told there might be better news if she came back in an hour or an hour and a half.

"How can I wait all that time?" she asked in pitiful tones.

"It's an eternity!" Nevertheless, she returned two hours later, and when the name which meant so much to her was not on the lists again, her composure gave way and she left the office sobbing.

Many of the women could not make themselves leave the office. They stood at the desk thinking in a kind of stupefaction.

One elderly woman leant against the staircase for support, and as tears coursed down her cheeks repeated: "He was a passenger, he was a passenger."

It was harrowing to see these people, who had fathers, mothers, sisters, wives and brothers aboard the Titanic. Inside the offices there was a strained atmosphere, a dreadful calm; people avoided each other's eyes and spoke in whispers.

Trembling fingers ran down the lists, followed by a gasp of relief or a sigh of pain at the presence or absence of names so eagerly sought.

On the sea of faces around the board could be detected joy, hope, anxiety and despair.

At the Leadenhall Street offices of the White Star Line there was a constant stream of men and women inquiring for the fate of their relatives and friends.

The vagueness and uncertainty of the published reports only added to the anxiety of the callers.

"If I could only know one way or the other!" was the cry made by most of the distracted relatives.

"I shall never see my son again," cried a mother whose 20-year-old son was aboard the Titanic.

By night the situation in the White Star Line's offices grew more and more tragic.

All day long many had waited, scanning each succeeding list of survivors with feverish hope, a few to go out into the world again aglow with new joy, but more destined to sink back in heavy despair until the next list fanned the smouldering hopes afresh.

33

The Daily Mirror

THE MORNING JOURNAL WITH THE SECOND LARGEST NET SALE.

No. 2,648. | Registered at the G.P.O. as a Newspaper | April 19, 1912 | One Halfpenny.

WHY WERE THERE ONLY TWENTY LIFEBOATS FOR 2,207 PEOPLE ON BOARD THE ILL-FATED TITANIC?

Something must be done by the Board of Trade to insist upon a larger number of lifeboats being provided for giant liners. Only twenty lifeboats were supplied by Messrs. Harland and Wolff for the Titanic, and even twenty, according to the Right Hon. A. M. Carlisle, the man who, as general manager to the company, was responsible for the building, was four in excess of the number required to comply with the Board of Trade regulations. "As ships grew bigger I was always in favour of increasing the lifeboat accommodation," said Mr. Carlisle, "yet it remains the same for a ship of 50,000 tons as for one of 10,000." The photograph shows the lifeboats on board the Titanic. It was taken while the giant liner was in Queenstown Harbour on Thursday of last week, in sight of land for the last time. Two boats, or even three if necessary, may be swung as easily as one on this type of davit. It will be seen that there is only one in the photograph.

NOT ENOUGH LIFEBOATS

TITANIC'S BUILDER BLAMES GOVERNMENT FOR INADEQUATE REGULATIONS

ONE of the most important questions which has been raised in consequence of the disaster is whether there were a sufficient number of lifeboats on the Titanic.

The Right Hon AM Carlisle, formerly general manager to Messrs Harland and Wolff, built the Titanic and partly designed her said yesterday that he did not consider the lifeboat accommodation required by the Board of Trade regulations was sufficient.

He said: "As ships grew bigger, I was always in favour of increasing the lifeboat accommodation. Yet it remains the same for a ship of 50,000 tons as for one of 10,000.

"When working out the designs of the Olympic and the Titanic I put my ideas before the davit constructors, and got them to design me davits which would allow me to place, if necessary, four lifeboats on each pair of davits, which would have meant a total of over 40 boats.

"Those davits were fitted in both ships. But, though the Board of Trade did not require anything more than the 16 lifeboats, 20 boats were supplied.

"The White Star Company did, of course, supply boats of very much greater capacity than those required by the Board of Trade. I think I am correct in saying that the provision, in cubic capacity, was practically double that which was required.

"At the same time, it was nothing like sufficient, in case of accident, to take off the majority of passengers and crew.

"I have no doubt that the government of this country, and the governments of other countries, will now look more seriously into the matter."

Above and opposite page: Amid the recriminations following the disaster, it soon became obvious that the limited number of lifeboats was the main reason for the deaths of over 1,500 people. Many more, if not all, could have been saved if the provision had been greater. The top picture shows one lifeboat alongside Carpathia, while immediately above is collapsible boat 'D', the last to leave Titanic

HUNDREDS OF FRIENDS AND RELATIVES ANXIOUSLY

Mr. B. Webb, a smoke-room steward on the ill-fated liner, and his young wife. It is not difficult to imagine the terrible suspense she is enduring.

Mr. W. White, one of the trimmers. He belongs to Southampton.

Mr. G. Kearl, a trimmer. Nothing is yet known of what became of him.

Mr. A. Stanbrook, a fireman. Like most of the crew, his home is at Southampton.

Mr. Sawyer, a cleaner, of Sou He has four youn

Miss Stella Sage, one of the family of eleven who are all missing.

This photograph, which has just come to hand, was taken on the Titanic—her deck can just be seen—by a passenger who travelled on her as far as Queenstown. It shows how nearly the ill-starred liner collided with the New York when see left Southampton on her fatal voyage. Alongside the Titanic is the Oceanic.

The Mackay-Bennett, whic search of bodies. Coffins balmers are on board.

"You're husband is saved," Lightoller is the

Mr. R. Bristow, third-class steward, photographed with his little child.

Mr. Sage, of Peterborough, who, with his wife and nine children, is missing.

Model of the davits as used on the Titanic. One, two or three boats can be attached to them, but in the case of the wrecked liner there was one boat per davit.

The davits in use. The photograph she

Mr. T. Hunt, a trimmer. Did he go down with the giant liner?

Mr. S. Williams, a trimmer, whose friends are anxiously awaiting news of him.

Mr. B. Coppenthwaite, one of the firemen. Is he among the saved?

Mr. J. O'Connor, a fireman. Is he among those of the crew who were rescued?

Mr. A. Dore, one of the trimmers. His friends waited for news for 4 days.

Father and son, Titanic. Both, too

An assortment of 30 faces, most of whom were crew members. At this stage their fates remained uncertain

FOR NEWS OF THE FATE OF THE TITANIC'S CREW.

W. Barrett, a fire-His fate is still a ter of conjecture.

Mr T. Preston, one of the trimmers, whose fate was uncertain.

Mr. C. J. Joughin, the chief baker, of whom news was anxiously awaited.

Mr. E. S. Freeman, a deck steward. What became of him is uncertain.

Mr. C. V. Clarke, one of the second-class passengers who is missing, and his wife, who is reported to have been saved.

the scene of the disaster in several undertakers and en-urch of England clergyman.

news in the world. Mrs. rescued officers.

Receiving a message yesterday in the London offices of Reuter, the newsagency which has supplied a large proportion of the news concerning the terrible disaster. The pneumatic tubes lead to the departments which communicate the news to the outside world.—(Daily Mirror photograph.)

Mr. E. N. Petty, a second-class bedroom steward. News of his fate is awaited.

has been launched while another is being ter.

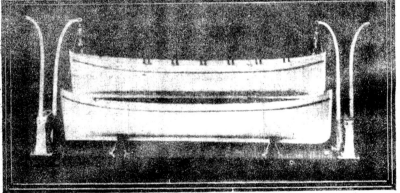
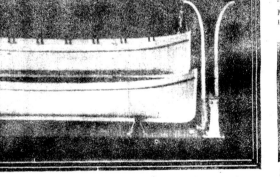

Three boats on the davits. The third one is in the background. The boats are about 30ft. long and carry between fifty and sixty passengers.—(Daily Mirror photographs.)

Mr. Reginald Barker, second purser, of whom nothing is yet known.

Mr. J. Chorley, a fireman. His friends have been torn with anxiety.

ere firemen on the W. May, strangely

Mr. W. Taylor, one of the firemen. Nothing is yet known of his fate.

Mr. P. Henry, a steward. Is he on board the Cunarder Carpathia?

Mr. Fred Banfield, of Helston, missing. He was returning from a holiday.

Mr. Harry Rogers, of Tavistock, an emigrant, who is missing.

Mr. J. P. Moody, one of the mates. He is a native of Grimsby.

The Daily Mirror

THE MORNING JOURNAL WITH THE SECOND LARGEST NET SALE.

No. 2,649.   Registered at the G.P.O. as a Newspaper.   SATURDAY, APRIL 20, 1912   One Halfpenny.

BANDSMEN HEROES ON THE SINKING TITANIC PLAY "NEARER, MY GOD, TO THEE!" AS THE LINER GOES DOWN TO HER DOOM.

NEARER, my GOD, to Thee,
    Nearer to Thee;
E'en though it be a cross
    That raiseth me;
Still all my song shall be,
Nearer, my GOD, to Thee,
    Nearer to Thee.

Though, like the wanderer,
    The sun gone down,
Darkness comes over me,
    My rest a stone;
Yet in my dreams I'd be
Nearer, my GOD, to Thee,
    Nearer to Thee.

There let my way appear
    Steps unto Heav'n,
All that Thou sendest me
    In mercy given,
Angels to beckon me
Nearer, my GOD, to Thee,
    Nearer to Thee.

Then, with my waking thoughts
    Bright with Thy praise,
Out of my stony griefs
    Beth-el I'll raise;
So by my woes to be
Nearer, my GOD, to Thee,
    Nearer to Thee.

When the historians chronicle the terrible disaster to the Titanic for the generations that have yet to be born, they will of a surety give the members of the orchestra a prominent place in the list of heroes. Though they knew that their minutes on earth were numbered, these brave men assembled on deck as the liner was going down and played "Nearer, My God, to Thee!" and it is easy to imagine the comfort that the music of this beautiful hymn must have brought to the unfortunate people who had to remain on the vessel. Miss Bonnell, an American survivor, relates this touching incident, and says that "by that time most of the lifeboats were some distance away, and only a faint sound of the strains of the hymn could be heard." Above are the words and music.

The Mirror of April 20 pays tribute to the bandsmen who, some claimed,
played 'Nearer, My God, To Thee' as the ship went down

Three decks of the Titanic are visible

CAPTAIN SMITH'S FATE ON THE DECK OF HIS SHIP

SUBLIME in its supreme unselfishness, the death of Captain EJ Smith was the death of an English captain – he perished with his ship.

Face to face with certain disaster, he was calm and self-possessed, thinking only of the lives of those in his charge. He ignored his own peril.

And then, when all that human foresight could do and had been done unavailingly to save the Titanic, he still remembered his quiet little band of hardworking officers, and released them from duty.

"It's every man for himself at such a time as this," he said. "I release you. Look out for yourselves."

But for Captain Smith there was no one to give the word of release. His place was with his riven vessel to the end.

Standing on the deck of his ship, alone, a solitary and heroic figure, Captain Smith faced death in the swirling ice-cold sea with all the calm, death-defying heroism that is the tradition of the men of the British Navy.

Poignantly sad in its realism is the word

picture of the passing of the Titanic's captain given by Mr George A Braden, of California.

He states: "I saw Captain Smith while I was in the water. He was standing on the deck all alone.

"Once he was swept down by a wave, but managed to get his feet again. Then, as the boat sank, he was again knocked down by a wave and then disappeared from view."

Extraordinary rumours cabled form America to the effect that Captain Smith shot himself as the Titanic was sinking, but this picturesque version was generally discredited yesterday.

Not the least of the heroes of the catastrophe were the Titanic's bandsmen.

In the whole history of the sea there is little equal to the wonderful behaviour of these humble players. In the last moments of the great ship's doom, when all was plainly lost, when presumably braver and hardier men might have been excused for doing practically anything to save themselves, they stood responsive to their conductor's baton and played a hymn, 'Nearer, My God, To Thee'.

THE FINAL SCENES OF TRAGIC HORROR ON THE SINKING TITANIC

THE humble truth of the catastrophe that overwhelmed the Titanic and carried 1,600 souls to their deaths is revealed in the vivid and awful accounts given by survivors.

Their narratives differ in many points of detail but in the main points there is for the most part agreement.

How no one realised what had happened

after the collision, how card-players resumed their play after a moment's interruption, how the men died like heroes, how the ship was blown in two by the explosion of the boilers and sank bows first – all this is told, together with stories of unspeakable horrors and sufferings and marvellous escapes and the heartrending sundering of brides from husbands.

The first reports that stated that Captain Smith shot himself dead on the bridge after a struggle with his brother-officers in the library is now discredited, and believed to have emanated from the hysterical imaginings of survivors overwhelmed by the horrors of the situation and confused by the chaos that surrounded them.

"GREATER LOVE HATH NO MAN THAN THIS, T

SOME OF THE MANY HEROES OF THE TERRIBLE TITANIC DISASTER WHOSE INDO

THE MOST AWFUL SHIPWRECK WHICH HAS

Mr. Harold Cottam, the Carpathia's wireless operator. He did not go to bed at the usual time on Sunday night, and as a result he caught the first message from the Titanic. This was responsible for saving hundreds of lives.

Mr. Jacques Futrelle, the well-known novelist, who, with Mr. W. T. Stead, displayed great courage in assisting in the preparation of the boats and helping the women.

Mr. J. P. Moody, one of the gallant officers of the Titanic who went down with the ship. Mr. Moody was a native of Grimsby. Four officers were saved.

Mr. Isidor Straus, the American millionaire. He and his wife were both drowned, Mrs. Straus refusing to leave her husband's side. According to the accounts furnished by survivors, this devoted couple went to their deaths together standing arm-in-arm on the first cabin deck.

Mrs. Isidor Straus.

Colonel J. J. Astor, the millionaire, who was drowned, and his young wife, who was saved. Survivors say that after embracing his wife, Mr. Astor stood erect and, with a military salute, turned back to his place in the sinking vessel.

Captain E. J. Smith, R.N.R., the veteran commander of now appears that he met his death like a true British sail a hero . . . He continued directing his men right up to

A gallery of heroes among officers from Titanic and Carpathia, who demonstrated "indomitable courage in the presence of death", foremost among them Captain Smith

MAN LAY DOWN . HIS LIFE FOR HIS FRIENDS."

OURAGE IN THE PRESENCE OF DEATH WAS THE ONE CONSOLING FEATURE OF URRED IN THE HISTORY OF NAVIGATION.

Mr. Phillips, the senior " wireless " operator, who sent calls for help while his assistant, Mr. Bride, fastened a lifebelt upon him. " Phillips was a brave man," said Mr. Bride.

Mr. Bride, who, though unable to walk owing to severe injuries to his feet, went on crutches to the relief of the overworked " wireless " operator of the Carpathia.

Captain A. H. Rostron, R.N.R., the commander of the Cunard liner Carpathia, which brought the survivors to New York. His was a terribly sad task, and the survivors speak of the "touching care and kindness" of both officers and crew.

Major Butt, an aide-de-camp to President Taft, who has been described as "the big hero of the disaster." "He quickly instituted a system to get the women off the liner, and he saw to it that the system was followed," said Mr. Daniel.

Mr. D. W. Marvin, of New York, who was drowned. His wife, who was saved, said: " As our boat shoved off he threw me a kiss, and that's the last I saw of him." The couple were returning home after a three-months' honeymoon trip in England.—(Dover-street Studios.)

Mrs. Marvin.—(Dover-street Studios.)

was at first reported, shot himself on the bridge. It f a survivor, he "stuck to the bridge and behaved like the bridge was level with the water."—(Daily Mirror

"FAITHFUL UNTO DEATH": "NO MAN JOSTLED A WOMAN

Mr. John Harper, pastor of the Walworth-road Baptist Chapel, who was drowned. He is seen with Miss Leitch, his niece, and his daughter Nana, who were both rescued by the Carpathia.

Mr. H. J. Pitman, third officer on the Titanic, who was one of the four officers saved from the wreck. Mr. Pitman, who is thirty-four years of age, is a native of Castle Cary, Somersetshire.

Mr. H. F. Lowe, the fifth officer, who is among the rescued. Mr. Lowe, who is twenty-nine years old, comes from Llandudno.

Mrs. Hurst, of 15, Chapel-road, Southam... that both her husband and father were los... surprise she received a telegram from N... Mrs. Hurst, who is seen with a baby in door. The portrait

Dr. J. Edward Simpson, assistant ship's surgeon, who went down with Dr. W. F. N. O'Loughlin, the senior surgeon.

Mr. Burke, one of the crew. A steward of his name appears on the list of those who have been rescued.

Sailors from the ships in port arriving for the Southampton memorial service.

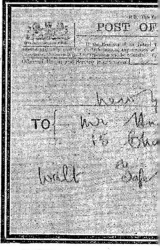

POST OF...

TO...

Mrs. Hurst's telegram. Scores of her...

"No American man jostled a woman or child as the weaker ones were hurried to the boats." This was the proud boast of Senator Smith, who is conducting the Tita...

Some more prominent figures who were on board Titanic, plus scenes from Southampton as people still struggle to come to terms with what had occurred thousands of miles away

LD AS THE WEAKER ONES WERE HURRIED TO THE BOATS"

Mr. Dyer, one of the engineers on board the Titanic, who perished in the disaster to the giant liner. In the event of a ship going down the engineers have a very poor chance of being rescued.

Mr. H. F. Wilde, the chief mate on board the Titanic, who went down with his captain. Mr. Wilde, who was thirty-eight years of age, belonged to Walton, Liverpool.

Mr. J. Wesley Woodward, 'cellist, and Mr. F. Clarke (double bass), who is seen in the circle. Their heroism in playing as the ship went to her doom is an incident which will live in history. Both belonged to Liverpool.

urday was bowed down with grief, believing
mourning for them. To her great joy and
ay saying: "Walt safe, father gone." Above,
reading the telegram to her aunt at her front
Daily Mirror photograph.)

GRAPHS.

SOUTHAMPTON

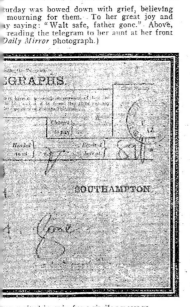

TITANIC DISASTER RELIEF FUND

Senator William Alden Smith, the chairman of the committee which is investigating the disaster in New York.

Mr. Frank Carlson, who was drowned. Formerly a ship's officer, he was returning to the States to settle.

ave waited in vain for a similar message.   Salvation Army band as it marched through Southampton collecting for the relief fund.

e headline above we purposely omit the word "American" because it is equally true of the Britishers aboard. The Anglo-Saxon race was triumphantly heroic to the last.

Right: Captain Rostron of Carpathia with a little girl who donated her spare clothes to children who survived

The Daily Mirror

THE MORNING JOURNAL WITH THE SECOND LARGEST NET SALE.

No. 2,651.   Registered at the G.P.O. as a Newspaper.   TUESDAY, APRIL 23, 1912   One Halfpenny.

THE SCANDAL OF THE LIFEBOATS: PUTTING MANY MORE ON THE OLYMPIC AFTER THE LESSON OF DISASTER TO HER SISTER SHIP.

Busy scenes were enacted on board the Olympic at Southampton yesterday. The lessons of the terrible disaster to her sister ship, the Titanic, are already being learned, and when she sails again to-morrow she will have on board no fewer than forty new lifeboats and collapsible boats and about a dozen rafts, which are in addition to the sixteen lifeboats she has hitherto carried. This means that there will be enough boats for everyone on board. (1) A lifeboat being hoisted on the giant liner. (2) Collapsible boats lying on the upper deck. (*Daily Mirror* photographs.)

The Daily Mirror

THE MORNING JOURNAL WITH THE SECOND LARGEST NET SALE.

No. 2,654.   Registered at the G.P.O. as a Newspaper.   FRIDAY, APRIL 26, 1912.   One Halfpenny.

FAMILY OF EIGHT, WHO WERE ON THE TITANIC BY CHANCE, ALL DROWNED IN THE DISASTER BECAUSE THERE WERE NOT ENOUGH LIFEBOATS.

Of the many sad cases of the Titanic disaster, few are more tragic than that of the Goodwins, of Kensington, all of whom were drowned. The family consisted of father, mother and six children, and it was only by chance that they were on the Titanic. They originally intended to sail during Easter week, but waited for the New York on account of the coal strike. At the last minute, however, they were transferred to the ill-starred liner. They were on their way to join Mr. Good-

win's brother at Niagara, where they intended to settle. (1) Mr. and Mrs. Goodwin and five of their children. (2) Sidney, the baby, aged eighteen months. (3) Mme. Navratil, of Nice, with her two children, who are believed to be Louis and Lolo, the French boys who were rescued. Mme. Navratil is certain they are hers, because of a number of coincidences she has noted. She is divorced from her husband, who took the children away.

The Daily Mirror

THE MORNING JOURNAL WITH THE SECOND LARGEST NET SALE.

No. 2,658.   Registered at the G.P.O. as a Newspaper.   WEDNESDAY, MAY 1, 1912.   One Halfpenny.

WOMEN PASSENGERS ON THE CARPATHIA CLOTHE AND TEND THE SURVIVORS OF THE TITANIC TRAGEDY.

When rescued from the Titanic lifeboats by the Carpathia many of the women were very scantily clad, as they had retired for the night when the giant liner crashed into the iceberg. This fact, of course, added tenfold to their sufferings as they drifted about in the piercing cold awaiting rescue. Once aboard the

Cunarder, however, everything possible was done for their comfort, passengers giving up their cabins and ransacking their trunks for clothes. The photograph shows women passengers sewing and distributing clothes. If the garments did not fit these kindly ladies took needle and thread and made the necessary alterations.

TITANIC INQUIRY OPENS IN LONDON TODAY

PROBABLY the largest array of counsel on record will attend the Board of Trade inquiry into the loss of the Titanic, which opens today under Lord Mersey at the Scottish Hall, Buckingham Gate.

The public will be admitted to the proceedings so far as the limited accommodation of the hall will allow.

These are the main questions which the court will attempt to solve:
- The seaworthiness and safety of the Titanic
- The circumstances leading to the wreck
- Whether there was any contributory default, and, if so, how and by whom
- What can be done to prevent similar disaster in future
- Changed regulations to the safety of human life on steamers

Special attention will be directed to the respective numbers of lost and saved in each class.

For the general convenience of the court, a large model of the liner has been prepared.

All the big shipping lines will be represented, as well, of course, as the Board of Trade.

Other parties to the inquiry will be the builders and the owners of the vessel, the surviving officers and the officers of some of the ships in the vicinity of the disaster.

Left and above: From mid-April and into May, the Daily Mirror's front pages were devoted to Titanic and its aftermath

Opposite page: The action moves into the courtroom as the official inquiries begin

Lord Mersey (right) oversaw
the Board of Trade inquiry
into the disaster

The Daily Mirror

THE MORNING JOURNAL WITH THE SECOND LARGEST NET SALE.

No. 2,656.   Registered at the G.P.O. as a Newspaper.   MONDAY, APRIL 29, 1912   One Halfp

MR. J. BRUCE ISMAY, CHAIRMAN OF THE WHITE STAR LINE, BEING CROSS-EXAMI
BY SENATOR SMITH BEFORE THE INQUIRY COMMISSION IN NEW YORK.

Scarcely had the Carpathia with her survivors of the Titanic catastrophe reached New York, than the Senate Investigating Committee held their first meeting at the Waldorf-Astoria Hotel. The first witness called was Mr. J. Bruce Ismay, the chairman of the White Star Line, who has been so much blamed in New York in connection with the disaster. Giving evidence on the first day, Mr. Ismay said that at the time he got into a lifeboat "there wasn't a woman on the b passenger of any class so far as I could see or hear." Above, M seen in the centre of the photograph with his hand to his chin, is evidence before the committee. He is also seen in the port Walery.)

The Daily Mirror

THE MORNING JOURNAL WITH THE SECOND LARGEST NET SALE.

No. 2,659.   Registered at the G.P.O. as a Newspaper.   THURSDAY, MAY 2, 1912   One Halfpenny.

THE BOARD OF TRADE INQUIRY INTO THE LOSS OF THE TITANIC
TO BE OPENED IN LONDON TO-DAY.

Captain A. W. Clarke.

Professor J. H. Biles, M.I.C.E.

Lord Mersey, who will preside over the inquiry.

Rear-Admiral S. Gough Calthorpe.

Commander F. C. Lyon, R.N.R.

Where the inquiry will be held. The portrait is of Mr. E. C. Chaston.

Titanic lifeboats at New York. They are all that remain of the vessel.

Why does nothing remain of the Titanic but a few lifeboats? The British inquiry into the loss of the world's largest liner will open to-day at the Scottish Hall, Buckingham Gate, when all the circumstances of the greatest wreck in history will be investigated. Lord Mersey will preside, and there will be five assessors, of whom portraits appear above. The public will be admitted as far as the accommodation will allow.—(Daily Mirror, Elliott and Fry, and Lafayette.)

Lookout Archie Jewell is the first person to give evidence to the British inquiry on May 3

MAY 4, 1912:

GRAPHIC STORIES BY SEAMAN AT TITANIC WRECK INQUIRY

YESTERDAY at the London Scottish Drill Hall the Titanic inquiry began in earnest, and extremely poignant evidence was taken.

Two seaman of the Titanic, Archibald Jewell and Joseph Scarrott, gave lucid and thrilling narratives of the last scenes on the doomed ship and the handling of the lifeboats.

On the night of Sunday, April 14 the atmosphere was clear – some witnesses said particularly clear.

The first witness, Jewell, of Bude, Cornwall, was a lookout man on the Titanic, and had been in the crow's nest from eight to ten on the fatal night with another seaman named Symons.

The men on duty took two hours each. As long as the weather was clear, only two men were on the look-out.

At 9.30pm a message was received on the bridge: "Keep a sharp look-out for all ice, big and small." Jewell thought it was the second officer who sent the message.

Up to that time they had seen no ice, and when he and Symons were relieved at ten o'clock by Fleet and Leigh he passed the message on to them, having seen no ice at all.

After he had turned in, he was wakened by a crash.

The second witness examined was Joseph Scarrott, an AB on the Titanic, whose voice was very clear but intensely dramatic and sometimes picturesque, as when he likened the fatal iceberg, as he saw it, to the Rock of Gibraltar.

He was at first given charge of No. 14 boat, and had on board 54 women, four children, two firemen and three or four stewards.

Scarrott's vigorous phrases, as when he spoke of "persuading" the men who tried to rush the boat on deck and throwing out three times a man who jumped in again and again, caused a titter in the hall, quickly checked of course, by the right feeling of all present.

He explained that some of the men who tried to rush the boat were foreigners, and could not understand what was said to them.

His account of the subsequent rescue of some of the floating survivors by his boat made the audience hold their breath.

One could almost see the mass of bodies floating on an ice-cold sea. It took half an hour to row a few yards to rescue a man praying and calling for help from a floating stairway.

He began his evidence from the dramatic moment at about 11.30pm when he heard three bells from the crow's nest.

"Then I felt a sort of shock," he went on. "Just as though the engines had been put full astern. It was the same sort of vibration, enough to make anybody wake up from their sleep."

Scarrott went on to state that the iceberg was about as high as the boat deck, 60 feet from the water. "It resembled the Rock of Gibraltar and was very much the same shape."

He went on to tell how he assisted with four boats before he joined his own boat, No. 14, on the port side.

He put himself in charge of the boat as the only sailorman there. After seeing that the boat was in order, he started to take the women and children into it.

"There were some men who tried to rush the boat, foreigners they were, because they could not understand the order I gave them. I prevented five getting in. One man jumped in twice, and I had to throw him out the third time.

"I told Mr Lowe, the fifth officer, I had had a bit of trouble in the rushing business and he said 'All right'. He pulled out his revolver and fired two shots between the the ship's and the boat's side and issued a warning to the remainder of the men about there. He told them if any more rushing took place, he would use it.

"No. 14 was then lowed into the water and we rowed clear of the ship. The ship sank after she broke in two, the stern remaining afloat for a couple of minutes after that, and then we all rowed to where she went down to see if we could pick up anybody."

MAY 15, 1912:

DRAMATIC MOMENTS AT
TITANIC DISASTER INQUIRY

THERE was a dramatic moment yesterday during the evidence before Lord Mersey's Titanic Wreck Commission.

One main point it was sought to establish, but at the end of the day the battle for the truth was still undecided. This was the question: Was the Californian the ship of the mystery lights which so many on board the Titanic say they saw a few miles distant when the liner had struck the iceberg?

There was a moment when the apprentice, James Gibson, seemed to be describing the going down of the Titanic as viewed from a vessel only five miles away, that he had unconsciously been a witness of the dread catastrophe that has wrung the emotions of a world of men and women.

The second officer and he were on the bridge of the Californian observing a vessel believed to be a tramp steamer.

They had seen rockets fired into the air from her direction, they had sent up Morse signals by lamp to which no answer came, they had wondered what the rockets meant.

Gibson, 20, said: "She seemed as if she had a heavy list to starboard." He was certain of this. Her port light, her red light, was higher in the water that it had been when he had first looked at the ship. Moreover, the white glaring lights seemed different somehow, although he could not explain how.

Yet further examination could not shake Gibson's conviction that the ship he had seen could not have been the Titanic but a steamer, and the second officer, who followed, was rooted in the belief that they could not have been gazing upon distress signals from the mammoth liner.

The Leyland liner Californian was said to have seen distress rockets fired from a vessel, which, according to a donkey-man, was the Titanic, and to have taken no notice of the signals.

Lord Mersey called Mr Stanley Lord, master of the vessel, and described how he arrived in the same icefield as the Titanic.

Close upon 11pm on the Sunday night he saw a steamer's light, but did not think it was the Titanic, and remarked so at the time. It was about six or seven miles away.

About 11pm he said to his Marconi operator: "Let the Titanic know that we are stopped – surrounded by ice." Lord continued to watch the approaching vessel until 11.30 when it stopped. It seemed to be a medium-sized ship, like his own.

The third officer attempted to communicate with it by Morse lamp, but got no reply. Captain Lord went to the chart-room shortly after midnight.

At 20 minutes to one he was told the Steamer was in just the same position, and at quarter past one the second officer reported that he had seen a white rocket.

Captain Lord, further examined, said the third officer stated that the vessel had two masthead lights.

Lord Mersey remarked: "That is important. The Titanic had two masthead lights."

Captain Lord pointed out that he and the second officer saw only one light. There were "any amount" of vessels with two masthead lights.

He did not hear at the time that the ship fired more than one rocket. He had since heard she did, and that the second officer sent a boy to call him. He remembered the boy coming to the chart-room, where he was lying down, but the lad said nothing. Not until 7am did he hear that several rockets had been fired.

He was under the impression that the rocket was not a distress signal, because, if it had been, the report would have been heard, the ship being only four or five miles away.

When he received a wireless message from the Virginian at 6am the next morning stating that the Titanic had stuck a berg and sunk, he proceeded to the scene.

The Attorney General asked: "Have you ever heard what the steamer was that sent up the rockets if she was not the Titanic?"

Captain Lord replied: "I have heard nothing about it."

AG: "Does it not strike you it must have been the Titanic?"

CL: "No, I am positive it was not. It would be utterly impossible for anybody to mistake the Titanic."

AG: "That would depend on the distance?"

CL: "You could not mistake it at four or five miles."

Captain Lord told Lord Mersey that the last seen of the ship sighted from the Californian was when she steamed away about 2am, going west and south-west. That was also the second officer's report.

Sir Cosmo Duff-Gordon, among the first to escape Titanic, gives evidence at the inquiry

READ ALL ABOUT IT!

With the 2012 centenary of the sinking of the Titanic on 15 April 1912 Haynes and The Daily Mirror have published **Titanic - The Unfolding Story**, to commemorate the fateful voyage that holds such a prominent place in history.

Titanic - The Unfolding Story captures the sequence of events as told in the Daily Mirror from the announcement that this ill-fated ship was to be built, through contemporary accounts of the disaster and all the inquests and stories that followed her sinking for years to come.

To order your copy at the exclusive special offer price of £14.99 plus P+P, call Haynes on:

01963 442 030 quoting reference 'MP'

JULY 31, 1912:

LESSONS OF THE TITANIC WRECK

NO sensational findings were provided in Lord Mersey's report on the Titanic disaster, which was delivered yesterday at the final meeting of the Commission.

In cold, unimpassioned phrase, the report sums up the greatest disaster of the sea, without bias or favour.

Lord Mersey himself read the report in the presence of a small assembly. Bruce Ismay, the managing director of the White Star Line, which owned the Titanic, was not present.

The main finding of the court was that:

The loss of the Titanic was due to collision with an iceberg, brought about by the excessive speed at which the ship was being navigated.

She was the largest passenger vessel ever built, and left Southampton, bound for New York, on Wednesday, April 10.

It was at 11.40pm on the following Sunday, April 14, that she struck an iceberg. There were 2,201 persons on board, of whom 711 were saved.

Lord Mersey's report says that the root reason why Captain Smith persevered in his course, and maintained his speed, is probably to be found "in competition and in the desire of the public for quick passages rather than in the judgement of navigators. Unfortunately experience appeared to justify it. In these circumstances I am not able to blame Captain Smith."

Lord Mersey's finding with regard to Captain Smith clears him of blame. The report says:

"He made a mistake, a very grievous mistake, but one in which negligence cannot be said to have had any part. It is, in my opinion, impossible to fix Captain Smith with blame. What was a mistake in the case of the Titanic would, without doubt, be negligence in any similar case in the future."

As to "the moral conduct" of Sir Cosmo Duff-Gordon and Mr Ismay, Lord Mersey says:

"The very gross charge against Sir Cosmo Duff-Gordon that, having got into No. 1 boat, he bribed the men in it to row away from drowning people, is unfounded."

Subject to the opinion that some of the boats might have attempted to save more lives, Lord Mersey has nothing but praise for both passengers and crew.

He regretted, however, that some boats failed to attempt to save life when they might have done so. This was particularly the case with No. 1 boat.

The No. 1 boat, it may be recalled, was that in which were Sir Cosmo Duff-Gordon and Lady Duff-Gordon.

Lord Mersey, dealing with the attack on Bruce Ismay, says: "I do not agree that any moral duty was imposed upon him to wait on board until the vessel foundered. Had he not jumped into the lifeboat he would merely have added one

Captain Stanley Lord (front, left) of the Californian poses with three senior officers. Lord was criticised for not coming to the assistance of Titanic

more life, namely his own, to the number of those lost."

Some of the salient features of Lord Mersey's report are as follows:

The evidence indicates to Lord Mersey that the rockets seen by the Californian came from the Titanic and no other ship.

The Californian could have pushed through the ice to the open water without any serious risk, and so have come to the assistance of the Titanic. Had she done so, Lord Mersey adds, she might have saved many, if not all, the lives that were lost. The Californian could have reached the Titanic if she had made when she saw the first rocket. She made no attempt.

A good and proper lookout for ice was not kept on board. "Without implying that those actually on duty were not keeping a good lookout, in view of the night being moonless – there being no wind and perhaps very little swell – and especially in view of the high speed at which the vessel was running, it is not considered that the lookout was sufficient."

At least eight boats did not carry their full loads because:

Many people did not realise the danger or care to leave the ship at first, some boats were ordered to be lowered with an idea of their coming round to the gangway doors to complete loading.

The officers were not certain of the strength and capacity of the boats in all cases.

The disproportion between the numbers of the passengers saved in the first, second and third classes is due to various causes, among which is the difference in the position of their quarters, and the fact that many in third class were foreigners.

The disproportion between the numbers of passengers and crew saved is due to the fact the crew for the most part all attended to their duties to the last, and until all the boats were gone.

Lord Mersey arrives at the Scottish Drill Hall on July 30, carrying his report

THE BITTER AFTERMATH

AFTER TITANIC SANK, MANY CERTAINTIES WERE SHATTERED. OVER 1,500 PEOPLE WERE DEAD, WHILE SOME CONTROVERSIALLY ESCAPED. THE INQUESTS INTO EVENTS QUICKLY BEGAN

RMS Carpathia docked at Pier 54 in New York following the rescue

AFTER the initial shock at the loss of Titanic had been absorbed, there was rising anger that basic failings had contributed to the scale of the disaster.

Just over 1,500 people died, leaving thousands of family and friends grief-stricken. Of those that survived, many lost loved ones. The "women and children first" policy meant there were significant numbers of passengers who were left without husbands or fathers.

The most glaring mistake was the lack of sufficient lifeboat provision. Titanic carried 20 rescue boats; 14 designed to carry 65 people each; two emergency boats (40 each) and four collapsable boats (47 each), giving a capacity of 1,178 seats – a shortfall of 1,050.

This was because the Board of Trade regulations only required a maximum of 16 for the largest of liners, believing that they would only be required to ferry those aboard to the rescue ships which, with the invention of wireless, would soon be on hand. Also, the owners wanted larger promenades to accentuate the opulence.

Of course, in the chaos and confusion, many of the boats were released short of capacity so the total of deaths was even higher than it should have been.

Among those who were tossed into the freezing ocean, around 50 managed to scramble into the last two collapsible boats. Very few others were picked up.

A graphic description of the tragic scene was given by Colonel Archibald Gracie, who jumped from Titanic as it went down and managed to cling on to the overturned collapsible boat 'B'.

He said: "There was nothing in sight save the ocean, dotted with ice and strewn with large masses of wreckage. Dying men and women all about me were groaning and crying piteously."

Gracie told afterwards that over half the men who originally managed to scramble aboard the boat were unable to hold on because it was so slippy, or succumbed to the freezing conditions. His own health suffered markedly because of hypothermia and he died before the year was out.

Smiles on the faces of
relieved survivors as
they reach dry land

Thomas Jones, an able
seaman from Anglesey, was
put in charge of lifeboat No. 8

Wireless operator
Harold Bride
scrambled onto a
collapsible boat

Colonel John Jacob Astor, the wealthiest man on board, with his young wife, Madeleine. He died, while she gave birth to his son four months later

Miraculously, chief baker Charles Joughin swam alongside a lifeboat and survived because, in his opinion, he had drunk so much alcohol it protected him from the freezing water.

Naturally, given the grandeur of the ship, there were plenty of wealthy people on board, including the Countess of Rothes and silent movie star Dorothy Gibson.

The richest was Colonel John Jacob Astor, 46, who owned sizeable chunks of Manhattan and was reputedly worth $87m.

He had just scandalised American society by marrying 18-year-old Madeleine Force, who was younger than his son and five months pregnant at the time of the voyage.

Madeleine escaped on boat No. 4, which was barely two-thirds full. Astor asked to be able to join his wife but the officer in charge stuck to the women and children rule.

His last act was to dash down to the dog kennels to free his Airedale, Kitty. Madeleine recalled seeing Kitty racing about on the sloping deck before they disappeared from view.

Astor's body was one of only 328 to be found (128 of them were unrecognisable). He was easily identified because his initials were on his shirt collar. On his body were his gold watch, gold and diamond cufflinks, a diamond ring, $2,440, £225, 50 French francs and a gold pencil.

Madeleine gave birth to a son, John Jacob Astor VI, on August 14.

Another wealthy American businessman, Benjamin Guggenheim, died in style. He was on board with his mistress, valet, chauffeur and his mistress's maid. He was initially dismissive of any danger, but after his female companions reluctantly boarded boat No. 9, the dreaded realisation began to dawn. Guggenheim and his valet returned to his cabin, dressed in evening wear and prepared to "go down like gentlemen". They were last seen in the staircase, sipping brandy and smoking cigars.

Isidor Straus, the owner of Macy's department store, watched boat No. 8 being loaded with his beloved wife, Ida. When Mrs Straus was offered a place in the boat, she declined, saying: "I will not be separated from my husband. As we have lived, so we will die, together."

An accompanying spot was then offered to Mr Straus, but he responded:

"No, I do not wish any distinction in my favour which is not granted to others."

Not everyone was so noble.

Sir Cosmo Duff-Gordon, who survived, was left a broken man because of stories about his behaviour during the rescue. He climbed aboard the first lifeboat with his fashion designer wife, Lady Lucile Duff-Gordon, and her personal maid, Laura Francatelli. There were only two male passengers and seven crew members alongside them. He offered £5 to each of the crew members. Although he claimed this was a reward for assistance, others saw it as a bribe to stop them going back for other passengers. Whatever the reality, the ensuing gossip broke his spirit.

Earlier in this magazine, we have already documented the similar notoriety that befell White Star chairman Bruce Ismay for boarding a lifeboat. His life was blighted forever from that point, as his actions were interpreted as selfish and cowardly.

Ismay received particularly stinging criticism from newspapers controlled by William Randolph Hearst, who had long disliked him. Ismay was said to be traumatised while on board Carpathia. At the US Senate inquiry, Charles Lightoller testified: "I may say that at that time Mr Ismay did not seem to be in a mental condition to finally decide anything. I tried my utmost to rouse Mr Ismay, for he was obsessed with the idea, and kept repeating, that he ought to have gone down with the ship because he found that women had gone down."

On April 23, Ismay sent a cable from New York to The Times newspaper in London, attempting to justify his escape from Titanic, and that of American first class passenger Mr Carter, in one of the last lifeboats.

It read: "I hope I need not say that neither Mr Carter nor myself would, for one moment, have thought of getting into the boat if there had been any women to go on it. Nor should I have done so if I had thought that by remaining on the ship I could have been of the slightest further assistance. It is impossible for me to answer every false statement, rumour or invention that has appeared in the newspapers."

In 1913 Ismay retired from the chairmanship of White Star and the International Mercantile Marine Company (IMMC). He had been due to retire as president of the IMMC but his request to stay on as chairman or director of White Star was rejected by the board. This ended the long involvement of the Ismay family in the direct management of White Star.

Captain Arthur Rostron (centre, seated) with his fellow officers from the Carpathia

Millvina Dean had the distinction of being the youngest passenger and oldest survivor. To the left, she is pictured in the Daily Mirror from May 13 1912. She was nine weeks old when the ship went down. Her family were emigrating to the USA, but returned to Britain as her father, Bertram, died in the disaster. Millvina died in May 2009, aged 97. Her ashes were scattered at Southampton docks by her long-time companion, Bruno Nordmanis (below)

One of the most pertinent facts about the sinking of Titanic was that a much higher proportion of the dead came from less wealthy passengers. The British Board of Trade inquiry concluded that 62% of first-class passengers were saved, 41% of second-class, 38% of third-class and 24% of the crew.

Titanic was designed to prevent the passengers in each class from mixing. Single male and female travellers were berthed at opposite ends of the ship and even as she was sinking, most of the barriers containing the passengers to their own class of quarters still remained.

The youngest person on board became the oldest survivor. Millvina Dean was a mere nine weeks old at the time of the sinking and was photographed in her mother's arms in the Daily Mirror in May 1912. She lived until May 31 2009, by which time she was 97. Her ashes were scattered in Southampton, from where Titanic set sail.

The human tragedies were plentiful. There were 20 newlywed couples aboard. Only one, the Bishops of Michigan, survived. In third-class, John and Annie Sage boarded with their nine children, while Fred and Augusta Goodwin came with six. None survived.

Thomas Hewitt, a bedroom steward from Liverpool, passed a watch to a stewardess shortly before his death. The watch was a present from his wife, Ada, dating from their wedding day 10 years earlier. The stewardess survived and was able to return the watch to Ada and their two children.

Eva Hart, pictured as a seven year old in 1912, survived alongside her mother, Esther (right). Her father, Benjamin (left), died. Eva is shown, at the top of the page, as an elderly woman, holding a Titanic book with Millvina Dean

Others were luckier. Rev J. Stuart Holden, vicar of St Paul's Church, Portman Square, London, was due to speak at a Christian Conservation Conference in New York's Carnegie Hall when his plans were halted by a sudden illness afflicting his wife. He cancelled the day before sailing. He is believed to have returned his first class contract ticket, but kept his boarding pass, which he later framed.

The senior officers who were in charge of Titanic experienced mixed fortunes. Captain Edward Smith went down with his ship, while Chief Officer Henry Wilde also perished. Wilde was off duty at the time of the collision, but took control of the even-numbered lifeboats on the port side. He was last seen trying to free the collapsible lifeboats.

First Officer William Murdoch gave the order to turn the ship immediately after the iceberg warning. He helped load women and children into the odd-numbered lifeboats but could not save himself. Controversially, James Cameron's 1997 film depicted him as panic-stricken and showed him shooting two passengers fighting for space in the boats before turning the gun on himself. After the movie's release, an executive from 20th Century Fox flew to Murdoch's home town of Dalbeattie in Scotland to apologise to family members for the erroneous portrayal.

Second Officer Charles Lightoller was the most senior surviving officer after managing to climb aboard collapsible boat 'B'. Fellow officers Herbert Pitman, Joseph Boxall and Harold Lowe also lived after being put in charge of lifeboats. Sixth Officer James Moody, who took the call from Fred Fleet warning of the iceberg, died.

A letter sent by a young girl, May Louise McMurray, on April 13 to her dad William, a bedroom steward, from Kensington, Liverpool. His body was never found. Below, two young survivors show no ill-effects

DX/1018/R
1989.192

60 Empress Road
Kensington
Liverpool
13.4.12

Dear Father
It seems ages since I last seen you. I wish we where in Southampton with you it is very lonely without you Dear Father I have not been so very well I have had a a bad throat hoping I will soon get better for Mana worried so much little Ernie as not been

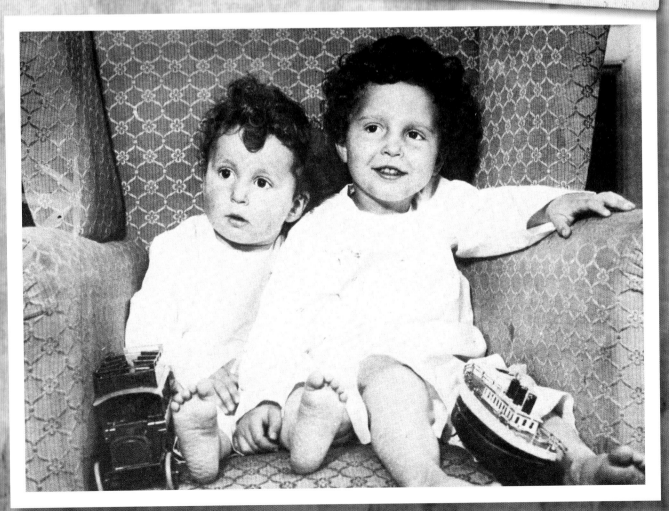

A kimono, complete with sea-sick vomit stains, worn by Lady Duff-Gordon on the night Titanic went down. Below, the Daily Mirror of April 18 pays tribute to WT Stead, a journalist who perished in the sinking

An apron worn by Laura Francatelli, the secretary to Lady Duff-Gordon. Picture courtesy: National Museums Liverpool

Fleet himself survived, as did his fellow lookout Reginald Lee. Radio operators Harold Bride and Jack Phillips both managed to scramble onto collapsible B but Phillips died after his health worsened during the freezing night.

The US Senate inquiry into the disaster opened almost immediately, on Friday, April 19, the day after Carpathia's arrival in New York. The hearings, which later moved from New York to Washington DC, took place over 18 days between April 19 and May 25. Apart from Bruce Ismay, four officers and 34 members of the crew were detained as possible witnesses.

The US inquiry reported on May 28. It made a number of recommendations for improving safety at sea, notably regarding the capacity and manning of lifeboats, boat drills, the provision of 24-hour wireless communication and the use of rockets at sea for distress signals alone.

In his summing up, Senator William Alden Smith, the inquiry's chairman, strongly condemned Captain Stanley Lord, master of the Californian, for his apparent negligence in failing to respond to Titanic's distress signals.

Medals were struck for Captain Rostron of the Carpathia, including the Congressional Gold Medal, the highest award the US could confer on him. Officers and crew members were also decorated with awards.

On Saturday, April 20 the remaining 172 crew members who had not been detained for the inquiry were allowed to leave for England on the Red Star Line steamer Lapland. Upon arriving in Plymouth on April 29, they were all herded into a third class dockside waiting room for the taking of depositions, or sworn witness statements, relating to the disaster. In addition, all had to appear before the Receiver of Wrecks before they could be released. This required them to stay overnight in the same waiting room, which had duly been equipped with bedding, tables and other basic facilities. The following afternoon they were allowed to leave for their homes.

Isidor and Ida Straus, who died together after Ida refused to get into a lifeboat without her husband

The official British inquiry into the disaster, set up by the Board of Trade, was held over 36 days between May 2 and July 26 under the Wreck Commissioner, Lord Mersey. A total of 48 former officers and crew of Titanic were summoned as witnesses.

The inquiry concluded that Titanic's loss was 'due to collision with an iceberg, brought about by the excessive speed at which the ship was being navigated.'

In considering what Captain Smith should have done, Lord Mersey observed that for at least 25 years liners using the same track in the vicinity of ice and in clear weather had kept to the course, maintained speed and kept a sharp lookout. This practice had 'been justified by experience, no casualties having resulted from it'. However, Titanic's loss had shown that this practice was 'bad'.

He continued: 'Its root is probably to be found in competition and in the desire of the public for quick passages rather than in the judgement of navigators.' With regard to Smith, the Commissioner concluded: 'He made a mistake, a very grievous mistake, but one in which, in face of the practice of past experience, negligence cannot be said to have had any part.'

The inquiry also found that a proper watch was not kept, that the ship's lifeboats were not properly manned and that there was no discrimination against third class passengers in the saving of life. Lord Mersey also severely censured the Board of Trade for its failure to revise the shipping rules of 1894 regarding lifeboat provision for the largest passenger liners.

Bruce Ismay was effectively exonerated regarding his moral conduct but Captain Stanley Lord was not so fortunate. Lord had argued that the steamer which approached Californian at about 11pm was too small to be Titanic. He said: "A ship like the Titanic at sea is an utter impossibility for anyone to mistake.'

However, the evidence of some of his crew contradicted him. Lord

Mersey, in his final report, stated that he was convinced by the evidence presented to him 'that the ship seen by the Californian was the Titanic and, if so, according to Captain Lord, the two vessels were about five miles apart at the time of the disaster. When she first saw the rockets, the Californian could have pushed through the ice to the open water without any serious risk and so have come to the assistance of the Titanic. Had she done so she might have saved many if not all the lives that were lost.'

Captain Lord's own verdict was that Lord Mersey 'had made up his mind before he started the inquiry, and was disinclined to listen to any further evidence.' His requests for a re-hearing of the evidence were refused. The Board of Trade decided not to prosecute him for allegedly failing to go to the assistance of a vessel in distress. Lord had been a witness at the inquiry, not a defendant, but if the board had attempted to withdraw his master's certificate he would have been able to call his own witnesses and cross-examine others.

After reading a review of 'A Night to Remember' in 1958, Lord's deep sense of injustice was reignited. He asked the Mercantile Marine Service Association (MMSA) to take up his case and finally clear his name. A long campaign ensued but without full vindication.

In 1965 and 1968 two detailed formal petitions were submitted by the MMSA to reopen the part of the 1912 inquiry which censured Captain Lord. These were rejected.

Leslie Harrison, an author and former general secretary of the MMSA, fought his case for 30 years. His book, 'The Titanic Myth', is dedicated to the captain, with the inscription: 'To the late Captain Stanley Lord, who endured a gross injustice with fortitude and dignity'.

Charles Lightoller, the most senior surviving officer, lived by clambering onto collapsible boat 'B'. At the top of the page is Ernest King, a clerk who was not so lucky

Harold Lowe, the only officer who, when in charge of a lifeboat, returned to Titanic after she sank, in search of survivors

HAROLD G. LOWE. 5th OFFICER ON R.M.S. TITANIC.
Born 1883. Died 1944.
'THE COOLEST HEAD OF ALL'

In his book, Harrison says the Californian shut down its engines at 10.15pm after becoming stuck in an icefield. The crew saw another ship several miles away but it was too small to be the Titanic and had only one masthead light. At 4.30am the crew was alerted to the Titanic's distress after a radio message. They set off towards the ship, which by now had sunk, but it took two and a half hours to get through the ice.

The mystery ship seen by the Titanic has never been accounted for. Captain Lord maintained until his death that his ship was at least 20 miles away.

There are many theories about why Lord did not go to the rescue of the Titanic, including that he was drunk. However, Lord's supporters believe he became a scapegoat because somebody had to take the blame.

A 1990-92 official reappraisal of the evidence produced ambiguous and inconclusive conclusions. Although it declared that the Californian had probably been between '17 and 20 miles from the Titanic', the opinions of the inspectors concerned were divided. On the one hand, the investigation found that Titanic's distress signals had been seen on the Californian and that no proper action was taken. On the other hand, it stated that any reasonable action

Below: Roberta Maoini, a maid who, aged 21, fell in love with a young steward while on board the liner. She survived but never saw the steward again, who was presumed dead. The tale had echoes of the love story in the 1997 movie. Above, right, is a copy of a poem she wrote about her lost love

by Captain Smith would not have led to a different outcome, since his ship would have arrived on the scene well after Titanic had sunk.

Despite retaining the full confidence of the Liverpool managers of the Leyland Line, Lord was soon forced to resign from his position with the company. He was informed that the board of directors in London had decided that public opinion was against him. Within a few months he had accepted a job as a master with the Nitrate Producers' Steamship Company of London.

He continued to command vessels until March 1927, when he was forced to retire due to poor eyesight.

After a century of argument, the culpability or otherwise of Stanley Lord for his actions that night remains in dispute.

The point of Titanic's rusted bow.
Picture courtesy: RMS Titanic Inc

THE SEARCH FOR TITANIC

SHE LAY UNDISCOVERED AT THE BOTTOM OF THE ATLANTIC OCEAN FOR 71 YEARS UNTIL AN
INTREPID AMERICAN FOUND HER IN 1985, SPARKING FRESH FASCINATION WITH THE LINER

IT was considered by many an impossible mission – locating the Titanic as she lay 13,000 feet below the surface of the Atlantic Ocean.

To find her would require boundaries to be pushed in deep sea exploration. Equipment had to be specially designed to withstand the water pressure at such depths.

Three times in the early 1980s Texas millionaire Jack Grimm headed an expedition which aimed to find her. Each time he failed.

Dr Robert Ballard, an oceanographer with the Massachusetts-based Woods Hole Oceanographic Institution, led a French-American research team who found the liner in Titanic in September 1985, 373 miles off Newfoundland. The wreck was in two sections with debris and possessions scattered over the ocean floor.

Dr Ballard met with the US Navy in 1982 to request funding to develop the robotic submersible technology he needed for the operation.

The military were interested in using the technology but only for inspecting two other wrecks – the submarines USS Thresher and USS Scorpion. They wanted to know the fate of the two nuclear reactors that powered the ships, and if there was any evidence to suggest that the Soviets had shot down Scorpion.

The Navy agreed to support Dr Ballard's expedition but made it clear that they were interested in studying the submarines. They reluctantly granted permission for him to go in search of the Titanic, but on the condition that time allowed after the sub mission had been completed.

In reality, the Navy did not believe he could find Titanic. If they had, permission may not have been forthcoming.

Dr Ballard found Thresher and Scorpion at depths of between 10,000 and 15,000 feet. His data showed the reactors were safe on the bottom of the ocean and were having no impact on the environment. Additionally, there was no evidence that an external weapon caused Scorpion to go down.

With only 12 days left in his mission, Dr Ballard went off in search of his real goal. While searching for the submarines, he noted how ocean currents affect sinking debris. He thus had an idea of how the Titanic's debris trail would appear on the sea bed. This information proved invaluable.

He utilised an unmanned submersible with built-in video cameras towed above the ocean floor at the end of fibre-optic wires.

After six days of looking at nothing but sand and mud, man-made ▶

The manned submersible Nautile
which recovered artefacts from
the seabed around the wreck in
1987. Picture courtesy: Ifremer

The bell rung by Fred Fleet
after the lookout spotted the
iceberg that doomed the ship

debris suddenly appeared. The Titanic had been discovered.

In a telephone interview with a Canadian television station later that day (September 1), he recalled the moment when it came into view.

He said: "We went smack-dab over a gorgeous boiler. I mean, it was straight out of all the books. We decided we would pull up and get above it all."

Dr Ballard said the initial excitement at discovering the rusted wreck had been replaced by the sobering realisation that "we had found the ship where 1,500 people had died".

They took 12,000 colour photographs of the area but did not retrieve any items that lay there – this first happened in 1987.

In 1994 a US court gave RMS Titanic Inc sole authority over the salvage and ownership of any artefacts recovered from Titanic. However, there are countless items that were brought to the surface before then which remain in general circulation. Auctions of Titanic possessions occur regularly, while other items are on public display in the Merseyside Maritime Museum, as well as Belfast's Transport Museum and Folk Museum. ►

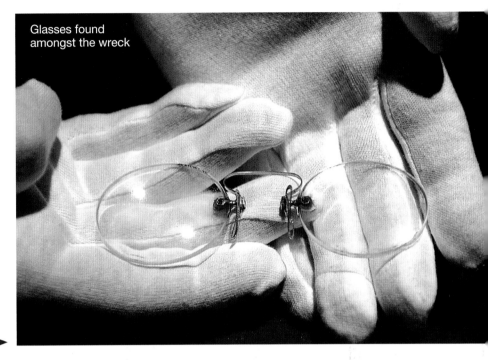

Glasses found amongst the wreck

Two bollards at the bow
showing the ravages of time

SEPTEMBER, 1985

THIS IS HOW THE DAILY MIRROR REPORTED THE DISCOVERY OF THE TITANIC, FEATURING THE REACTION OF A SURVIVOR:

RAISE THE TITANIC...OR SHOULD SHE BE LEFT TO REST IN PEACE?

AND at last we see her, after all these years. Huge. Ghastly. Still.

Lying where she came to rest after slowly tumbling down through 13,000 feet of freezing water.

All 46,000 tons of her.

Even in the thick night of the Atlantic bottom, eerily slit open by the spotlight, there is no mistaking the massive presence of the Titanic's hull.

There are sights down there that are even more arresting, say the survey team who have located the wreck of the luxury liner 400 miles off Newfoundland.

A deck bench recovered from the wreck. Picture courtesy: National Maritime Museum

A porthole and, above, a watch, both recovered from Titanic

A £5 note found on the sea bed

When she hit the iceberg and sank, she was a floating palace of luxury, bedecked with millionaires and lovely ladies, fine crystal and rare wines, delicate china and elegant furniture.

And you can see it, say the team who are probing the wreck with their robot sub. There in the black and the slime.

Unbroken dinner plates. Cases of claret. Bowls, basins and chamber pots.

No doubt, if the little robot probes long and indiscreetly enough, the very instruments of the band who carried on playing while the ship went down. But one of the few remaining survivors of the sinking says the wreck should be left in peace.

Miss Eva Hart, aged 80, from Chedwell Heath, looked at the picture and for the first time saw her father's grave.

She recalled the agony of watching him prepare to die when she was a seven-year-old being put in a lifeboat with her mother.

Benjamin Hart told his daughter: "Be good. Be nice to Mummy." Then he went down with the 'unsinkable' Titanic, he and 1,500 others.

Miss Hart said: "Nobody should ever attempt to raise that ship. It's like robbing a grave.

"We watched that magnificent ship going down. I didn't sleep all night. To hear people drowning is a dreadful sound.

"I think the people died unnecessarily. They wouldn't have if there had been enough lifeboats.

"It was a tragedy of tragedies."

She added: "I have great admiration for the scientists who have found her – but everyone should leave her where she is."

The US-French team who found the ship have no plans to attempt to raise her but other groups have said the operation could be attempted.

It is a measure of just what a hold the Titanic still has on our imaginations.

To the people of 1912, the sinking was more than just a major civil disaster.

They were an optimistic generation and it shook their world rigid. It was like something out of the Bible.

Even 73 years later, in our Godless age, we are haunted by the image of the great ship, and the greater-yet floating mountain of ice that sealed its doom.

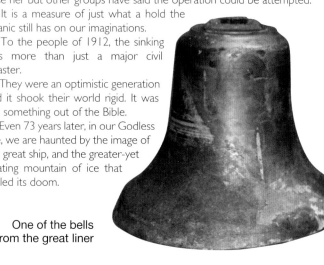

One of the bells from the great liner

Rows of dishes lying on the sea bed

IN FILM AND ON SCREEN

THE STORY OF THE TITANIC HAS PROVED IRRESISTIBLE TO MOVIE STUDIOS AND TELEVISION COMPANIES OVER THE YEARS, MOST NOTABLY THROUGH JAMES CAMERON'S 1997 EPIC, STARRING KATE WINSLET AND LEONARDO DI CAPRIO. AS THE ANNIVERSARY APPROACHES, ANOTHER BIG-BUDGET PRODUCTION IS IMMINENT, PLUS AN AMBITIOUS PIECE OF STREET ART

Actor Kenneth More shakes hands with Mr S Daniels of Portsmouth, a Titanic survivor, at the premiere of 'A Night To Remember at the Odeon, Leicester Square, July 1958. More played Charles Lightoller in the film

Kate Winslet with two Empire Film Awards, including Best Actress, for
Titanic. Below, her co-star Leonardo Di Caprio meets Prince Charles in 1997

William Murdoch: 20th Century Fox had to apologise for the way he was portrayed in the 1997 movie

AS the National Museum Northern Ireland website puts it, "The story of Titanic combines money, power, ambition and pride, with love, courage, loss and redemption. In fact, it contains all the ingredients for a dramatic screenplay."

This has been proved on many occasions over the years, as the tale has been repeatedly documented and/or dramatised for cinema and television. The appetite shows no sign of being sated.

In 2012 ITV are to broadcast a four-part mini-series written by the man behind Downton Abbey, Julian Fellowes. Called, somewhat predictably, 'Titanic', it is billed as a "new retelling of the doomed voyage" featuring a combination of historical and fictional characters.

The series will feature approaching 100 actors and will explore the stories of many of the people who were on board, rather than focusing on two central characters.

Actors starring in Titanic include Linus Roache, Celia Imrie, Toby Jones, Geraldine Somerville, Sophie Winkleman and Timothy West. It is due to be broadcast over four nights, from April 12-15.

There is also a HBO-funded television drama due for broadcast. 'Titanic: Blood and Steel' is a 12-part serial based around the construction and subsequent sinking of the ship. Part of it has been filmed in Northern Ireland. Among the featured actors are Derek Jacobi, Neve Campbell and Chris Noth.

Of course, when it comes to Titanic productions the grandaddy of them all remains, and possibly always will be, James Cameron's 1997 record-breaker.

It set new standards for special effects and sets, helped in no small part by a budget of $200m.

The film was centred around a fictionalised love story between Rose DeWitt Bukater (Kate Winslet) and Jack Dawson (Leonardo Di Caprio). Cameron believed the film needed a love story to help modern audiences relate to the actual event, although some felt it was unnecessary.

Genuine historical figures were also part of the story, including Bruce Ismay, Captain Smith and Colonel JJ Astor.

Director Cameron was inspired to produce a Titanic film because of his fascination with shipwrecks. He ventured down to the seabed to film the wreck, which helped kick-start filming.

The actual production was not without its problems, as Cameron's demanding nature caused tensions between him and the actors on set, with many cast members becoming ill after spending hours in cold water during filming.

A full scale model of the ship was built and it was placed within a 17-million gallon water tank. The sets depicting the interior rooms on board were reproduced exactly as the originals using photographs and original plans from Harland and Wolff.

It was released in December 1997 and proved a commercial and critical success, grossing $1.8m worldwide. It was the first film to garner over a billion dollars and remained the highest grossing film in history until Cameron's follow-up, 'Avatar', was released in 2010.

Titanic received an incredible 14 Academy Award nominations and won 11 Oscars, including Best Picture and Best director. Although, in some quarters, it has become unfashionable to praise the film in the years since its original release, the reality is that the vast majority of the audience loved it.

When it was released on VHS in the UK, 1.8m copies were bought in the first week, smashing the previous record. It also became the first DVD to sell 1m units at a time when the discs were new to the market.

It is about to break more new ground through being released in 3D this spring, a perfect fit for the anniversary.

As has been stated earlier, one negative was the way First Officer William Murdoch was portrayed. The film makers, 20th Century Fox, apologised to his descendants for suggesting he was a coward.

Cameron himself said what happened to Titanic was perfect for cinema. "The story could not have been written better," he said. "The juxtaposition of rich and poor, the gender roles played out unto death (women first), the stoicism and nobility of a bygone age, the magnificence of the great ship matched in scale only by the folly of the men who drove her hell-bent through the darkness. And above all the lissom: that life is uncertain, the future unknowable…the unthinkable possible."

It has been suggested that James Cameron was inspired to make Titanic after seeing the 1958 British film 'A Night to Remember'.

Based on Walter Lord's book of the same name, it has a good reputation and generally stayed faithful to the story, without too much elaboration or decoration. The budget was £500,000, a huge sum for the time.

Kenneth More, its main star, played the ship's second officer, Charles Lightoller, who was depicted as a heroic figure responsible for saving a significant number of lives.

BBC History magazine views A Night to Remember favourably: "The film dramatises the night's tragic events without ever becoming overwrought. We see the tremendous faith in the 'unsinkable' ship, the unheeded ice warnings, ice falling on deck at the moment of impact, 'women and children first' in the lifeboats…it is a judicious account."

There have been many other films based on what happened to Titanic, but these are the two most successful. There was one produced in Germany in 1912, the year Titanic went down. One of the more well known was an American production in 1953 (the first to be simply called 'Titanic') starring Robert Wagner.

However, none come close in scale or ambition to Cameron's blockbuster.

Left: James Cameron, who directed the 1997 epic, with Sigourney Weaver

Below: Julian Fellowes, the man responsible for Downton Abbey, is providing the script for the new drama

Linus Roache, who is starring in the 2012 ITV drama

Chris Noth and (top picture) Neve Campbell on set in Dublin while filming scenes for 'Titanic: Blood and Steel'

This giant girl puppet will parade through the streets of Liverpool from April 20-22 as part of three days of street threatre to commemorate the Titanic anniversary. The event will be produced by French company Royal De Luxe

The stunning centrepiece of Belfast's Titanic Quarter

A CENTURY ON – STILL THE MOST FAMOUS SHIP IN THE WORLD

A VARIETY OF EVENTS AND EXHIBITIONS WILL MARK THE TITANIC CENTENARY, AS THOUSANDS OF PEOPLE FLOCK TO REMEMBER A SHIP THAT HAS A PERMANENT HOLD ON THE IMAGINATION

THE anniversary of the disaster is a landmark moment in Britain, with events planned in the three cities most closely tied to the ship, Belfast, Liverpool and Southampton.

It has been the catalyst for a major regeneration project in Northern Ireland's capital, with the 'Titanic Quarter' due to open on March 31 on the site where the liner was built.

The centrepiece is a stunning building, 'Titanic Belfast', that will house a huge, permanent exhibition devoted to all things Titanic. It will feature nine galleries and make use of special effects, dark rides, full-scale reconstructions and interactivity to tell the story from construction and launch to the sinking and controversial aftermath.

A Titanic Light Show will take place between 7 and 11 April, when the ship's story will be projected on to the new building via digital mapping.

Across the Irish Sea, Merseyside Maritime Museum will be staging its own exhibition, 'Titanic and Liverpool: The Untold Story', opening on March 30. This will focus on the city's role in the incredible tale.

Ian Murphy, curator of maritime history with National Museums Liverpool, is expecting half a million visitors for their exhibition, which is initially due to run for a year.

He said: "We are featuring some rarely-seen items from our collection to explore Liverpool's role in the ship's story, particularly the Liverpool people who were involved.

"Titanic appeals to people for many reasons. It's such a strong human tragedy. It also represents the opulence of the Edwardian era and the high point of the British empire.

"It was a huge engineering achievement and it was all undermined by something as simple as an iceberg. The loss of the Titanic was a real shock, which cut across all parts of society. It had a huge effect on the lives of so many men, women and children."

In Southampton, the SeaCity Museum is due to open while an evening of music is being staged at the Southampton Guildhall on the evening of April 14, the night when the iceberg was struck.

While there appears to be an emphasis on the spectacular in all three cities, it will inevitably be a time for reflection as people remember those who were lost, particularly ancestors who were on board.

Why, after all this time, is there such a fascination with this particular ship? Simply, she was the biggest, the most beautiful, the most luxurious, the most ambitious liner ever built. It lacked for nothing, apart from the necessary safety provisions.

She set sail backed by the belief that man and modern technology could triumph over nature and the sea. Sadly, a shuddering reality check lay in its path.

Just weeks before the anniversary, the risks inherent in sea travel were brought into sharp focus by the disaster that befell the Costa Concordia after it hit rocks off the coast of Tuscany, in Italy.

In echoes of what happened to Titanic, passengers were forced to flee the liner in lifeboats moments after they had been enjoying dinner and drinks in the ship's bars and restaurants. Most of the 4,200 on board made it to shore but, at the time of writing, 15 were confirmed dead with a further 25 missing.

As for the grandaddy of them all, Titanic's hold on the imagination is demonstrated whenever any items related to the ship come up for auction. The interest is huge, and frequently so are the sums paid for various trinkets and treasures.

Meanwhile, huge visitor numbers are expected at the various Titanic exhibitions opening this year.

It may have sunk on its maiden voyage, but Titanic is the ship that never disappears from view.

Right: A statue of Captain Edward Smith overlooks Beacon Park in Lichfield

Titanic looms imposingly in the background as shipyard workers leave Queen's Island, Belfast, at the end of a working day in May 1911. This was days before its launch

The great liner stands tall and proud.
It might be a century since she sank,
but Titanic's fame never fades

WHITE STAR LINE.

"OLYMPIC."
45,000 TONS.
AND
"TITANIC."
45,000 TONS.

THE LARGEST STEAMERS
IN THE WORLD.

ALL STEAMERS BUILT IN IRELAND.

QUEENSTOWN–NEW YORK
ON THURSDAYS AND FRIDAYS.

QUEENSTOWN–BOSTON
ON WEDNESDAYS.

For Freight and Passage apply to

JOHN DENNEHY,

Insurance Agent, CAHIRCIVEEN, Co. Kerry.

THE LIVERPOOL PRINTING & STATIONERY C° LIMITED.